THE BEIRUT MASSACRE

THE BEIRUT MASSACRE

The Complete Kahan Commission Report

with an introduction by
ABBA EBAN

KARZ-COHL
Princeton · New York

Published in the United States of America
by Karz-Cohl Publishing, Inc.
First edition, 1983.
Introduction copyright © 1983 by Karz-Cohl Publishing, Inc.
All rights reserved under international and
Pan-American copyright conventions.
Printed in the United States of America.

English language translations of the September 22, 1982
parliamentary speeches by Defense Minister Ariel Sharon and
Labor party leader Shimon Peres are reprinted by permission
of The New York Times, Copyright © 1982 by The New York Times
Company.

ISBN 0-943828-55-4
1 2 3 4 5 6 7 8 9 0

KARZ-COHL PUBLISHING, INC.
320 West 105th Street, New York, N.Y. 10025

INTRODUCTION
Abba Eban

THE BACKGROUND

At the beginning of June 1982 few people in Israel had ever heard of Sabra and Shatilla, of Alei and the Shuf Mountains, of Amin Jemayel and the Shi'ite community in Jabal Amal. There was no premonition that these remote and exotic words would come to fill the minds and emotions of Israelis and all who cherished Israel's cause and that they would totally convulse our nation's scale of priorities for months to come. If a spokesman for the Israeli government in the first week of June had declared that the country had never been more secure or so little exposed to violence, it would have been hard to deny the claim. There was tranquility on every side. The border with Egypt was serene in the shelter of the peace treaty concluded in March 1979. There had been no turbulence from Jordan since 1970, when King Hussein had expelled the PLO from the soil of his kingdom. Syria was full of militant and vengeful rhetoric, but there had been not a single act of violence since June 1974, when a disengagement agreement had been negotiated with Israel through the mediatory efforts of Secretary of State Henry Kissinger. That agreement had been meticulously observed by both parties for eight years and showed no sign of erosion. Syria, under President Hafiz el Asad, had been able to combine militant rhetoric with careful discretion. Even the northern border with Lebanon had been tranquil for nearly a year. In July 1981, after a series of small-scale but ominous acts of violence that had taken its toll among Israeli civilians and had led to Israeli bombing of Beirut, a cease-fire had been obtained through the

---

ABBA EBAN, formerly Ambassador of Israel to the United States and the United Nations, and Minister of Foreign Affairs, is currently a member of the Israeli Parliament (Knesset) and the spokesman of the opposition Labor party on foreign affairs in the Knesset.

good offices of President Reagan's emissary, Ambassador Philip Habib. The agreement was theoretically concluded between Israel and the government of Lebanon, but the real interlocutor on the Arab side was the PLO. Lebanon had not sent terrorists into Israel and did not need to cease fire which it had never opened. By the beginning of June 1982 the inhabitants of Galilee and other northern regions had been able to live, breathe, and move freely without constant fear of the "terror that walketh by night."

And yet the problem of the northern border had not been "settled." The PLO was not striking, but its capacity to strike made life for many Israelis like sitting on a volcano: even when there was no eruption, the possibility of an outbreak of violence hung broodingly in the air. A cease-fire is always a trade-off: in return for the absence of fire each party gives the other an uninterrupted capacity to fill its armories and to plan its future action. Reports reaching Israel from the north were mixed: some described the PLO as regrouping and preparing for a wave of violence, while others conveyed the impression that the PLO was petrified by fear of Israeli reactions, which it had no real power to repel or absorb. In particular, the PLO leadership was aware of the vulnerability of its bases and headquarters in Beirut to Israeli air attack. It was unlikely that anyone in Arafat's entourage would want to raid northern Israel without also "wanting" to have Beirut bombed.

The two alternative appraisals of PLO intention were matched by two conflicting attitudes in the Israeli political system. One viewpoint held that the cease-fire was tenuous, provisional, and, perhaps, even harmful since it enabled the PLO to grow stronger without fear of harassment. This view was strongly held in the top army command and was known to be shared by Defense Minister Ariel Sharon. The other view was that while a cease-fire lasted it ought to be preserved, since nothing is inevitable until after it has occurred and since whatever deterrents and restraints had prevented PLO violence for a year might well exist undiminished for another year and, therefore, for a third and fourth. Just as there is a dynamic in war, so is there a dynamic in an absence of war. When the disengagement agreement had been signed with Syria in 1974 few were optimistic enough to predict eight uninterrupted years of tranquility; yet this had ensued. The spokesmen for this "wait and see" approach included the leaders of the Labor party. During the month of May and up to June 1, the Israeli press was carrying articles and interviews from General Yitzhak Rabin, General Chaim Barlev, and the party leader Shimon Peres expressing reservations about any despatch of Israeli forces to Lebanon for military action unless or until a major

VI

provocation came from the PLO itself. Peres, Barlev, and Rabin are three names without which no one can write the history of Israel's defense establishment. Peres had been minister of defense, Rabin had been chief of staff and, later, prime minister, and Barlev had been Israel's senior tank commander before becoming chief of staff after the Six Day War of 1967. With this massive military authority on their shoulders the Labor trio had personally told Prime Minister Menachem Begin of their belief that the peace of Galilee should be assured by the cease-fire, supplemented by convincing deterrent strength.

Deterrence is the key word. Here we come up against a doctrinal conflict that has split Israel and the Zionist movement down the middle for half a century. It concerns the question of armed force in the solution of the national predicament, more particularly, the predicament created by Arab hostility. From the outset, the Labor movement, which established the Israel Defense Forces under David Ben Gurion's leadership in 1948, was not a pacifict movement. Faced by an implacable and ferocious Arab hostility with genocidal overtones, to have denied the principle of armed resistance would have been to invite the victory of aggression. To be a pacifist in the Middle East is to have an interesting but brief existence. Yet the classical Israeli approach to armed force was always restrained. Golda Meir had spoken of the doctrine of "ein brera"—war when there is no choice; war when you must, not when you can; war as the last, reluctant resort when all other possible remedies have been exhausted. This implies a reactive approach whereby war is chosen only when an attack has been launched or is clearly imminent. Under this traditional doctrine Israel has been willing to make war only when a refusal to make it would have endangered its territorial integrity, its sovereignty, or the lives of its inhabitants.

A corollary of this reactive approach has been a principle of limited war. This involves using less than one's total power to achieve something less than the total destruction of the adversary. Israel's wars always ended when it would have been physically possible to push the fighting further. Behind these restrictive criteria lies a cautious or pessimistic view of what war can achieve when it goes beyond its preventive function. War can prevent; it cannot create. It can prevent an enemy from destroying your life and home and thus enable history to continue on its course. But it cannot construct new textures of relationship or create the harmonies and mutual interests necessary for the establishment of a new and better international order. This means that it must be replaced and succeeded as soon as possible by politics and diplomacy, which move by persuasion, not coercion.

Before the establishment of the Israeli state, this classic Israeli doctrine about the relationship between war and politics was challenged by the Zionist Revisionist movement, out of which Menachem Begin's Likud government would later emerge. The revisionist view gave war a larger place, created a mystique of heroism, and during the 1930s and 1940s attached great weight to martial songs, uniforms, parades, and unofficial armies. In the movements of resistance that preceded the independence of Israel, the small revisionist groups were less fastidious than the larger official Zionist forces in their manner of combat. They did not shrink from personal assassinations and attacks on predominantly civilian Arab targets. When Israel became a state under Labor governments, the opposition, led by Menachem Begin, supported all the wars that Israeli governments felt forced to make and strongly advocated wars that Israeli governments refused to make.

Against this historic background it becomes easier to understand why the major political groups in Israel reached different conclusions about what to do on the Lebanese frontier in June 1982. The unambitious advice of the Labor leaders was to maintain the cease-fire as long as possible and to conduct a limited operation for the removal of PLO weapons and personnel from the range of Israeli villages if it became evident that the cease-fire had failed.

The design adopted by Menachem Begin and Defense Minister Ariel Sharon was far less inhibited. The first decision was not to put any further faith in the cease-fire but to strike across the frontier at a suitable time, irrespective of whether the PLO in Lebanon initiated a breakdown of the cease-fire or not. The immediate target would be to push the PLO out of a belt of territory 40 kilometers wide that runs parallel with the Israeli-Lebanese boundary so as to insure that no PLO fire could reach Israeli land or lives. On June 8, Mr. Begin informed the Labor leaders privately and the Knesset publicly that once this objective was achieved "all fighting would cease." If that had occurred the war in Lebanon would have ended after the first five days, during which Israeli forces, vastly superior in numbers and equipment, had cleared the PLO out of the security belt to Israel's north, demolished the Soviet-made missiles that Syria had installed in the Beka'a valley, and brought down 90 Syrian aircraft with the loss of two Israeli planes! There had been some 60 Israeli casualties at that time.

It is a moot point whether Mr. Begin himself believed this limited version of the Galilee operation. (It would later emerge in the Kahan commission report that the defense minister had the custom of taking major operational decisions without informing the prime minister). What is certain is that a local operation was never any part of Mr. Sharon's thinking, nor did it figure in the calculations of the chief of staff, Lieutenant General Rafael Eitan. They saw the move into Lebanon on June 6 as the first phase in a great design that would radically change the Middle Eastern scene and Israel's place within it. They envisioned a wide range of repercussions resulting from the war, and the Israeli people and the world would hear a great deal of them in the ensuing months:

- The PLO would be physically destroyed in Lebanon and would cease to be an influential actor in regional politics;
- Free of the intimidation of PLO terror the Palestinian Arabs in the West Bank and Gaza would come forward and negotiate agreements on the basis of the Camp David agreement as interpreted by Mr. Begin (autonomy as a prelude to permanent incorporation into Israel);
- A stable, strong government would arise in Lebanon capable of extending its authority over the whole country;
- A Lebanese president would be elected with a commitment to conclude a peace treaty with Israel by the end of 1982;
- There would be free movement of people and goods from Egypt across Israel to Lebanon, creating a "triangle of peace" as a basis of a new regional order;
- The United States would rejoice in Israel's defeat of the pro-Soviet PLO and Syria, and a better relationship would develop between Israel and America;
- Security arrangements would be agreed in South Lebanon enabling close Israeli participation in the policing of the area to insure absolutely that no mortar bomb or grenade could ever come within range of an Israeli life or home;
- There would be a sharp reduction of Soviet involvement and influence in the Middle East.

Nine months later not one of these objectives has been achieved. Yet there was a moment of euphoria in August 1982, when it seemed that many parts of this blueprint would come to fruition. By the end of the month the terrorists had been evacuated from Beirut and a multinational force composed of units from the United States, France, and Italy had nervously taken up their positions. Arafat himself had been compelled to leave the city in which he had been the virtual overlord, commanding an army that might seem trivial according to Israeli dimensions, but which was sufficient to overawe and dominate the Lebanese, who had virtually become guests in their own country. Bashir Jemayel, the leader of the

Christian Phalangists, was about to become president of Lebanon. He had maintained close relations with Israeli leaders since the days of the Rabin government, and these links had been strengthened in a common front against the PLO and Syria, whom the Phalangists correctly diagnosed as the enemies of a separate Lebanese nationalism. The United States had been opposed to the initial Israeli thrust across the frontier on June 6. The war had, in fact, begun two days previously, when the ambassador of Israel to Britain, Shlomo Argov, had been shot in a London street by a small group of Palestinian terrorists; he had sustained grievous and permanent injury. The next day, Israeli aircraft bombed Beirut with heavy loss of Arab life, and the PLO responded by firing mortar and artillery shells into Galilee villages, causing no fatalities but exposing the intrinsic vulnerability of the population. The crime of which the ambassador had been the tragic victim had little relevance to the problem of Israel's northern frontier, since his assailants belonged to an Iraqi-based splinter group that was just as violently opposed to Arafat and the main body of the PLO as it was hostile to Israel. The United States had urged the maintenance of the cease-fire and had adjured Israel not to march, but when the campaign had been launched with impressively rapid results, the American reaction became resigned and even had a tinge of buoyancy: United States representatives emphasized that even if unfortunate events had taken place they may have created "opportunities" for a better situation than that which had existed before.

All in all, the atmosphere surrounding the Israeli campaign on September 1 had not been excessively abrasive. The memories of the bombardment of Beirut during July and August had injured the image of Israel as a humane democracy, and such episodes as the denial of water to the city in the heat of summer had evoked strong protests in Israel itself. But some of these impressions had been softened by the recollection of great cruelties inflicted on the Lebanese nation by the PLO before the Israeli invasion had even been conceived, and the hope that a new and better order of relations might be built on the debris of the war was shared by many who would not have advocated the war in the first place. In Israel itself a great majority of the public expressed itself in polls in support of the war as a successful venture likely to achieve its goals. The reservations came from those sensitive to moral issues and, surprisingly, from important elements of the armed forces. This was a sensational and ominous development in terms of Israeli history. Officers expressed tormenting doubts both about the propriety of exposing Israeli soldiers to death for issues quite remote from the "peace of Galilee" and about the fact that thousands of civilians, Palestinian and

x

Lebanese, had been killed in operations designed to eliminate a relatively small number of terrorists. Great public tension had been roused by the resignation of an Israeli war hero, Colonel Eli Geva, the nation's senior tank commander, who had refused to cooperate with an operation that could lead to a frontal assault by the Israel Defense Forces on West Beirut with certainty of heavy loss of life both among Israeli troops and among Lebanese and Palestinian civilians, including children. But by and large, if the situation had been stabilized on September 1, the Israeli people would have absorbed the shock and turmoil of the war with none of the anguish by which it was now to be convulsed.

September was the tragic month. Nothing much had gone wrong in August, and nothing at all was to go right in September. The turning point was the assassination of president-elect Bashir Jemayel on September 14. He had led a violent life marked by internecine rivalries that had torn Lebanon for all his thirty-seven years. It was a sign of the times that there were at least four plausible theories about who might have put him to death. Nobody will ever know if he would have fulfilled the hopes that Begin and Sharon had reposed in him as a leader who would sign a peace treaty with Israel and risk the consequent fury of the Arab rejectionists in Syria, Saudi Arabia, and among the Palestinians: at a meeting with Israeli leaders in Safed a few days before his death he had shown signs of retreating from the more fulsome promises that he had made, and it was reported that Begin and his colleagues had spoken sharply with him. But there can be no doubt that he was more likely than any other Lebanese leader to strengthen his links with Israel and enable the Israeli government to emerge with clear gains after the sacrifice of the battlefield. If not for Israel's campaign the Phalangists would never have got anywhere near the seats of power, and Bashir would never have won the presidential election, which had been conducted in the Lebanese parliament a few yards from Israeli tanks and guns.

THE CRISIS

The death of Bashir Jemayel sent shock waves throughout the Middle East. The immediate prospects were dark. There was a likelihood of a new bloodbath in Lebanon in the wake of a constitutional crisis and the resurgence of all the vengeful passions engendered by an unfinished civil war. The PLO might take a new lease on life now that their most rigorous Lebanese adversary had fallen. And for Israel, especially Menachem

Begin and Arik Sharon, the structure of hopes laboriously built throughout the summer months might collapse like a house of cards. If Israeli war aims had been confined to the clearing of the 40 kilometer belt mentioned by Prime Minister Begin on June 8, the changes of leadership in Beirut might not have been momentous. But by September the war had ceased to be a war for the peace of Galilee alone and had become a war of Lebanese independence in which Israel had high stakes. For good or ill, Israel had become involved in Beirut as intimately as any nation can in the fate of a neighbor, and it was in an atmosphere of alarm that two decisions were taken in Jerusalem that would reverberate throughout the ensuing months.

On September 15, at 6:00 AM, Israeli forces entered West Beirut, where they encountered no resistance. The government announcement said that the purpose was "to prevent possible grave occurrences and to ensure quiet." The decision was taken by the prime minister and defense minister without discussion or vote in the Cabinet.

On September 16, at about 18:00 hours, the Phalangists entered the Shatilla refugee camp and later moved into the Sabra camp. This decision was taken by Defense Minister Sharon and Chief of Staff Rafael Eitan without informing the prime minister, who heard of it the next day together with other Cabinet members after the fact of the entry. The Cabinet gave retroactive consent to the decision.

The above two decisions and their consequences continue to reverberate in the political life of Israel and the Middle East and in the arenas of world opinion. They took the war into a phase that had never been conceived before. The domestic effects were grave. The Labor opposition, which had not been consulted on any of the operative stages of the war since June 10, dissociated itself from both decisions. "Why did you take the crazy decision to let the Phalangists into the Palestine refugee camps?" asked the opposition leader Shimon Peres in an impassioned address to the Knesset. The question was to resound in Israel and the world for many months.

The decision to enter West Beirut had its chief repercussion in the field of American-Israeli relations. The United States was in a relatively relaxed frame of mind until that time. Its role in evacuating the terrorists from Beirut had been appreciated by Israelis and by Lebanese nationalists. It had brought particular credit to the president's emissary, Philip Habib. But with most of the able-bodied menfolk out of the camps the United States felt a direct responsibility for the women and children left behind in the camps and was perturbed that the Israeli entry might lead to a recrudescence of fighting with the remnants of the PLO forces and the

Moslem militias (Mourabitoun). President Reagan and Secretary of State Shultz expressed vigorous protest to Prime Minister Begin, both publicly and through diplomatic channels. Their assumption had been that the Lebanese war had reached a territorial standstill with Israeli forces outside the perimeter of West Beirut, where the institutions of the Lebanese government and most of the foreign embassies were concentrated. The multinational force, led by the American contingent of marines, had precipitately left the country some days before; this was felt at the time, and turned out subsequently, to have been a bad and hasty decision. But the argument between Washington and Jerusalem about the Israeli entry into West Beirut was soon eclipsed by a greater clamor when it became evident that the Phalangists had carried out a gruesome pogrom against undefended civilians in Sabra and Shatilla. Official Israeli estimates would put the number of those killed at something between seven and eight hundred. The details of the murders themselves, of the terrifying ordeals of the victims, of the Nazi-like sadism with which the Phalangists did their work, of the vain effort of women and children to escape from the camps, which were surrounded by Israeli troops, all added up to a horror story, enhanced in the world's imagination by the macabre images of the corpses projected on the world's television screens and in the mass-circulation weeklies.

It was later published in many Israeli newspapers and speeches that the media had ignored the fact that the actual killing had been done by Lebanese Phalangists, not by Israelis. This is not accurate. I have not seen a single report that failed to attribute the slaughter to the Lebanese Phalangists. But they are a vague, new, unfamiliar concept to world opinion: they have never sought or obtained the legitimacy or sanction of the outside world. They have not been actors in the universal drama, and their very obscurity and irrelevance gave them shelter from the censure of the world. Most of the immense eruption of public comment and argument centered on Israel's role. Were the Israeli soldiers in the vicinity merely by chance or were they, inconceivably, in liaison or contact with the Phalangists or even in some posture of command? The question gnawed at the very roots of Israel's conscience, and within a few days it was plain that without some great cathartic release the question would have a stifling effect. Israeli life simply could not go on unless the release was sought.

To understand why this was so one must take certain attributes of Israeli society into account. Israel has been the only country in the world that has never known a month of peace in all the years of its national existence. It has faced the question of physical survival with every nightfall and every rising dawn. It would therefore seem to have less need than any other nation to defend its obsession with physical protection. Yet whenever Israelis talk of war and peace they talk in terms of right and wrong. The moral preoccupation gives a special pathos and nobility to Israeli life; and at the center of Israel's image of itself stands the Israel Defense Forces as the exemplar of those virtues that have not been swamped by the ethos of a pragmatic, modern, consumer society—the bright memory of ancient valor and modern sacrifice. It was vital to cleanse the army of any doubt, whether by confession, by acquittal, by inquiry, or by the clear attribution of responsibility. It was in that atmosphere that the inquiry commission was born.

It was the work of the Israeli people, not of the governmental establishment. Four hundred thousand Israelis demonstrated in Tel Aviv calling for an independent inquiry into Israel's role in the events of September 16–18. President Yitzhak Navon, in an unusual departure from the noncontroversial nature of his office, made a similar appeal; Mr. Begin's initial reaction was so insensitive that Israeli public opinion could not sustain it. Indeed, if the governmental response had been different at the outset, the public and international disquiet might have been contained with lesser commotion. The inquiry commission makes this point with great cogency:

> When a public furor erupted in Israel and abroad in the wake of the reports about the massacre . . . several communiqués were issued by the IDF and the Foreign Ministry which contained incorrect and imprecise statements about the events. These communiqués asserted explicitly or implied that the Phalangists' entry into the camps had been carried out without the knowledge of—or coordination with—the IDF. The incorrect statements were subsequently amended, and it was stated publicly that the Phalangists' entry into the camps had been coordinated with the IDF. *There is no doubt that the publication of incorrect and imprecise reports intensified the suspicions against Israel and caused it harm* [emphasis added].

The commission was convinced that a harsh truth is more salutary than a smooth evasion. Its words lie before the reader, and they spare no truths. The massacre is the direct responsibility of the Christian Phalangists, but since the Israeli army controlled their entry into the camps, provided them with services, including illumination at night, and knew at an early stage that they were functioning in violation of humane principles, there is an indirect Israeli responsibility. The commission rejects the government's claim that the massacre was such a surprising development that those who ordered the Phalangists into the camps could not reasonably have predicted the massacre. It believes that the massacre was a logical development of the decision to introduce the Phalangists into Sabra and Shatilla. It accuses Defense Minister Sharon and Chief of Staff Rafael Eitan of failure to discharge their duty and recommends a discontinuation of their leadership of the defense establishment. It charges the prime minister himself with being apathetic, uninterested, lacking in foresight and vigilance, and being uninvolved to such a degree as to impose on him "a measure of responsibility." It expresses shock at the fact that Foreign Minister Yitzhak Shamir received authentic news of the massacre from a cabinet colleague and failed to act on that news in any way, thus missing a chance for the government to intervene at an earlier stage. It finds a lack of professional vigilance or normal concern in the actions of some army officers of high rank. In a lucid and eloquent summary the commission implicitly rejects the contention that such criticism of official Israeli actions might have adverse effects on Israel's position or repute:

> The main purpose of the inquiry was to bring to light all the important facts relating to the perpetration of the atrocities; it therefore has importance from the perspective of Israel's moral fortitude and its functioning as a democratic state that scrupulously maintains the fundamental principles of the civilized world.

The report does not make a judgment on the Lebanese campaign as a whole. When it was written, the verdict on the overall balance of gain and loss was in suspense, as it remains. The tone of the report gives more support to the critics of the later phases of the war than to those who applaud every stage in the campaign. But the basic justification of Israel's right to protect itself against PLO terrorism is strongly endorsed. If Lebanon had been left alone by the PLO, and if the PLO had not made the Palestinian refugees the instruments of an aggressive design, the tragic chain of events that reached its climax in mid-September 1982 would never have begun. Israel has laid the burden of self-criticism upon itself, while the chief agents of the tragedy—the PLO and the Christian Phalangists—have gone their way in callous indifference. So the story ends in moral paradox—for everyone concerned except the nation for whom the commissioners spoke.

CONCLUSION

In the final reckoning Israel has emerged with pride and credit from this report. The credit is shared by public opinion, the opposition, which called for the inquiry, by the Begin government, which agreed to appoint it and to abide by its conclusions, and by the three eminent Israelis who gave eloquent expression to a moral preoccupation for which it is hard to find a parallel in the practice or tradition of any other modern state. The inquiry commission electrified world opinion and filled the media with words of respect and admiration for the Israeli nation. Very few countries would allow their actions to be scrutinized and criticized with such relentless truth and rigor. Countless people across the world who had not been able to identify with Israel's policies were able to admire the fact that those policies were under meticulous analysis in Israel itself so that the outside world had no need, or right, to make itself the forum for scrutinizing Israel's conduct. The commission evidently has contempt for the view that public criticism of Israeli policies can harm Israel's image or interests. On the contrary, it obviously believes that it is more important and credible to change policy by criticism than to promote policy uncritically. Indeed, it is the statement on the critical function in a democracy that makes this document so primordial and significant a contribution to democratic jurisprudence. The underlying philosophy of its approach is based on a realistic diagnosis of mankind's political nature. Nobody who has great authority can be trusted not to go beyond its proper limits. There is a kind of aesthetic beauty in the democratic structure that finds a restraint or a balance for every contingency of authority pushed too far or power deployed without a sense of harmony.

Three thousand years ago King David, having performed a spectacularly unworthy crime, received a visit from the prophet Nathan, who denounced his monarch with searing rhetoric: "Thou art the man." In ancient civilizations there is no parallel to this Hebrew notion of a ruler being subject to a law, as though he were his own subject. In other parts of the Middle East a swift and agonizing death would be the fate of anyone who laid doubt on royal infallibility. The appeal to a tribunal of conscience that stands above and apart from power is part of the prophetic tradition. It is only thus that power is humanized by being brought under the covenant of reason and law.

PUBLISHER'S STATEMENT

The text of the Kahan commission report herewith printed was taken from the original *Final Report* document, which was released in Israel on February 8, 1983. Changes have been made only regarding factual errors, mistranslations (which were noted in the *Jerusalem Post*), typos, and inconsistency in the upper and lower casing of certain words. Otherwise, we have not in any way altered the text as it is set out in the original document.

CONTENTS

THE BEIRUT MASSACRE

THE COMMISSION OF INQUIRY
INTO THE EVENTS AT THE REFUGEE CAMPS
IN BEIRUT

1983

FINAL REPORT

(AUTHORIZED TRANSLATION)

YITZHAK KAHAN, President of the Supreme Court, Commission Chairman

AHARON BARAK, Justice of the Supreme Court

YONA EFRAT, Major General (Res.), Israel Defense Forces

INTRODUCTION

At a meeting of the Cabinet on 28 September 1982, the Government of Israel resolved to establish a commission of inquiry in accordance with the Commissions of Inquiry Law of 1968. The Cabinet charged the commission as follows:

"The matter which will be subjected to inquiry is: all the facts and factors connected with the atrocity carried out by a unit of the Lebanese Forces against the civilian population in the Shatilla and Sabra camps."

In the wake of this resolution, the President of the Supreme Court, by virtue of the authority vested in him under Section 4 of the aforementioned law, appointed a commission of inquiry comprised as follows:

Yitzhak Kahan, President of the Supreme Court, commission chairman; Aharon Barak, Justice of the Supreme Court; Yona Efrat, Major General (Res.).

The commission held 60 sessions, hearing 58 witnesses. As per the commission's requests of the Cabinet Secretary, the Office of the Minister of Defense, the General Staff of the Israel Defense Forces (henceforth, the I.D.F.), the Ministry for Foreign Affairs, and other public and governmental institutions, the commission was provided with many documents, some of which were, in the course of the deliberations, submitted to the commission as exhibits. The commission decided, in accordance with Section 13(A) of the law, that there was a need to

1

collect data necessary for its investigation. Appointed as staff investigators were: Ms. Dorit Beinish, Deputy State Attorney, and Ms. Edna Arbel, Senior Assistant to the District Attorney (Central District), who were seconded to the commission by the Attorney General; and Assistant Police Commander Alex Ish-Shalom, who was seconded to the commission by the Inspector General of the Israel Police. Judge David Bartov was appointed commission coordinator. The staff investigators collected, by virtue of the authority vested in them under Sections 13(C), 180 statements from 163 witnesses. Before the commission began its deliberations, it visited Beirut, but it was not allowed to enter the area of the events. The commission also viewed television footage filmed near the time of the events at the camps and their surroundings.

The commission published notices to the public in the press and other media, inviting all who wish to testify or submit a document or bring any information to the commission's attention to submit to the commission in writing details of the material he possessed or wished to bring to the commission's attention. There was not much response to these appeals. The commission made an effort to collect testimony also from people who live outside the juridical boundaries of the State of Israel; and all necessary steps were taken to bring witnesses from outside of Israel, when this was possible. The commission's requests in this matter were not always honored. For example, the *New York Times* correspondent Mr. Thomas Friedman, who published in the aforementioned newspaper a detailed article on what transpired during the period under deliberation here, refused to appear before the commission, claiming that this was contrary to his paper's editorial policy. We did not receive a satisfactory answer as to why the paper's publisher prevented its reporter from appearing before the commission and thus helping it uncover all the important facts.

Some of the commission's hearings were held in open sessions, but most of the sessions were in camera. In this matter we acted in accordance with the instructions of Section 18(A) of the law, according to which a commission of inquiry is required to deliberate in open session but is entitled to deliberate in camera if it is convinced that "it is necessary to do so in the interest of protecting the security of the State . . . the foreign relations of the State . . ." and for other reasons stipulated in that section. It became clear to the commission that with regard to certain matters about which witnesses testified before it, open hearings would be liable to affect adversely the nation's security or foreign relations; and therefore it heard most of its testimony in camera. It should be noted that during sessions held in camera, witnesses also said things whose publication would not cause any harm; however, because of the difficulty in separating those things whose publication would be permissible from those whose publication would be forbidden, it was imperative in a substantial number of cases to hear the entire testimony in camera.

In accordance with Section 20(A) of the law, this report is being published together with an appendix that will be called Appendix A. In the event that we will need recourse in this report to testimony whose publication would not be damaging to the nation's security or foreign relations, we shall present it in a section of the report that will be published. On the other hand, in accordance with Section 20(A) of the law, a portion of this report, to be called Appendix B, will not be published, since, in our opinion, non-publication of this material is essential in the interest of protecting the nation's security or foreign relations.

As we have said, the commission's task, as stipulated by the Cabinet's resolution, is "to investigate all the facts and factors connected with the atrocity which was carried out by a unit of the Lebanese Forces against the civilian population of the Shatilla and Sabra camps." These acts were perpetrated between Thursday, 16 September 1982, and Saturday, 18 September 1982. The establishment of the facts and the conclusions in this report relate only to the facts and factors connected with the acts perpetrated in the aforementioned time frame, and the commission did not deliberate or investigate matters whose connection with the aforementioned acts is indirect or remote. The commission refrained, therefore, from drawing conclusions with regard to various issues connected with activities during the war that took place in Lebanon from 6 June 1982 onward or with regard to policy decisions taken by the Government before or during the war, unless these activities or decisions were directly related to the events that are the subject of this investigation. Descriptions of facts presented in this report that deviate from the framework of the commission's authority (as defined above) have been cited only as background material, in order to better understand and illustrate the chain of events.

In one area we have found it necessary to deviate somewhat from the stipulation of the Cabinet's resolution, which represents the commission's terms of reference. The resolution speaks of atrocities carried out by "a unit of the Lebanese Forces." The expression "Lebanese Forces" refers to an armed force known by the name "Phalangists" or "Keta'ib" (henceforth, Phalangists). It is our opinion that we would not be properly fulfilling our task if we did not look into the question of whether the atrocities spoken of in the Cabinet's resolution were indeed perpetrated by the Phalangists, and this question will indeed by treated in the course of this report.

The commission's deliberations can be divided into two stages. In the first stage, the commission heard witnesses who had been summoned by it, as well as witnesses who had expressed the desire to appear before it. The commission asked questions of these witnesses, and they were given the opportunity of bringing before the commission everything known to them of the matters that constitute the subject of the investigation. When this stage terminated, the commission issued a resolution in accordance with Section 15(A) of the aforementioned law, concerning the harm that might be caused certain people as a result of the investigation or its results; this was done in order to enable these people to study the material, to appear before the commission and to testify (for the text of the resolution, see Section 1 of Appendix A). In accordance with this resolution, the chairman of the commission sent notices to nine people; the notices detailed how each one of them might be harmed. The material in the commission's possession was placed at the disposal of those receiving the notices and of the attorneys appointed to represent them. During the second stage of the deliberations, we heard witnesses who had been summoned at the request of the lawyers, and thus some of the witnesses who had testified during the first stage were cross-examined.

Afterwards, written summations were submitted, and the opportunity to supplement these summations by presenting oral arguments was given. We should already note that involving the lawyers in the commission's deliberations did not in any way make the commission's work more difficult; it even helped us in fulfilling our task. The lawyers who appeared before us were able to clarify properly, though not at excessive length, the various points that were the subject of controversy; and thus they rendered valuable assistance to the commission's task, without in any way prejudicing their professional obligation to properly represent and defend their clients.

When we resolved to issue, in accordance with Section 15(A) of the law, notices about harm to the nine people, we were not oblivious to the fact that, during the course of the investigation, facts were uncovered that could be the prima facie basis for results that might cause harm to other persons as well. Our consideration in limiting the notices about possible harm to only nine persons was based on [the conception] that it is our duty, as a public judicial commission dealing with an extremely important issue—one which had raised a furor among the general public in Israel and other nations—to deliberate and reach findings and conclusions with regard to the major and important things connected with the aforementioned events, and to the question of the responsibility of those persons whose decisions and actions could have decisively influenced the course of events. We felt that with regard to the other people who were involved in one way or another in the events we are investigating, but whose role was secondary, it would be better that the clarification or investigation, if deemed necessary, be carried out in another manner, and not before this commission, viz., before the military authorities, in accordance with the relevant stipulations of the military legal code and other legislation. We chose this path so that the matters under investigation would not expand and become overly complicated and so that we could complete our task in not too long a time.

In the course of the investigation, not a few contradictions came out regarding various facts about which we had heard testimony. In those cases where the contradictions referred to facts important for establishing findings and drawing subsequent conclusions, we shall decide between the variant versions in accordance with the usual criteria in judicial and quasi-judicial tribunals. Our procedures are not those of a criminal court; and therefore the criterion of criminal courts that stipulates that in order to convict someone his guilt must be proven beyond a reasonable doubt, does not apply in this case. Nevertheless, since we are aware that our findings and conclusions are liable to be of significant influence from a social and ethical standpoint, and to harm also in other ways persons involved in our deliberations, no finding of significant harm was established with regard to any one of those to whom notices were sent, unless convincing evidence on which to base such a finding was found, and we shall not be satisfied with evidence that leaves room for real doubt. We shall not pretend to find a solution to all the contradictions in testimony. In many instances, these contradictions relate to the content of conversations that took place between various people without the presence of witnesses, or when the witnesses' attention was not focused on the content of the conversation, and there are no exact notes on these conversations. In such cases, it is only natural that there exist several versions with regard to what was said, and the differences between them do not necessarily derive from a desire to conceal the truth but rather are sometimes the natural result of a failure of the human memory. We do not see the need to rule about those contradictions which surround unimportant details that do not influence the decision about points in controversy.

We shall conclude this part of the report by expressing appreciation and gratitude to all those who helped us in fulfilling our task. It is only fitting that we note that all the institutions and various functionaries in the Government, the I.D.F., and other authorities whose help we needed rendered us all the necessary assistance and placed at our disposal all the

5

relevant material, without reservation. Our special thanks go to the coordinator of the commission, Judge David Bartov, who showed great capability in handling the administrative aspects of the commission's work and without whose enterprise and devoted and efficient work it is very doubtful whether we would have succeeded in properly carrying out our task. Our appreciation and gratitude go also to the staff investigators, Dorit Beinish, Edna Arbel and Alex Ish-Shalom, who, by virtue of their expertise, initiative and dedication, succeeded in placing at our disposal much material which served as the basis of the commission's deliberations and findings. Similarly, our thanks go to the entire staff of commission employees, whose loyalty and faithfulness enabled us to carry out and complete our task.

A DESCRIPTION
OF THE EVENTS

The Period Before
the Events in Beirut

In 1975, civil war broke out in Lebanon. This war began with clashes in Sidon between the Christians and Palestinian terrorists and subsequently widened in a manner to encompass many divers armed forces— under the auspices of ethnic groups, political parties, and various organizations—that were active in Lebanon. In its early stages, this war was waged primarily between the Christian organizations on the one hand, and Palestinian terrorists, Lebanese leftist organizations, and Muslim and Druze organizations of various factions on the other. In the course of the civil war, Syrian army forces entered Lebanon and took part in the war, for a certain period of time on the side of the Christian forces, and subsequently on the side of the terrorists and the Lebanese leftist organizations. During the early years of the war, massacres on a large scale were perpetrated by the fighting forces against the civilian population. The Christian city of Damour was captured and destroyed by Palestinian terrorists in January 1976. The Christian residents fled the city, and the conquering forces carried out acts of slaughter that cost the lives of many Christians. In August 1976, the Christian forces captured the Tel Za'atar refugee camp in Beirut, where Palestinian terrorists had dug in, and thousands of Palestinian refugees were massacred. Each massacre brought in its wake acts of revenge of a similar nature. The number of victims of the civil war has been estimated at close to 100,000 killed, including a large number of civilians, among them women and children.

6

The Palestinians' armed forces organized and entrenched themselves in camps inhabited by refugees who had arrived in Lebanon in various waves, beginning in 1948. There are various estimates as to the number of Palestinian refugees who were living in Lebanon in 1982. According to the figures of U.N.R.W.A. (the United Nations Relief and Works Agency), the Palestinian refugees numbered approximately 270,000. On the other hand, the leaders of the Christian armed forces estimated the number of Palestinian refugees at approximately 500,000 or more. This estimate is most probably exaggerated, and the more realistic estimate is the one that puts the number of Palestinian refugees at approximately 300,000—and in any case, not more than 400,000.

The main Christian armed force that took part in the civil war consisted mainly of Maronite Christians, though a small number of Shi'ites joined them. This force comprised several armed Christian organizations, the largest among them being the organizations under the leadership of the Chamoun family and of the Jemayel family. The head of the Jemayel family, Mr. Pierre Jemayel, founded the Phalangist organization; and the leader of this organization in recent years was Pierre's son, Bashir Jemayel. In the course of time, the Phalangist organization became the central element in the Christian forces; in 1982, the Phalangists ruled the Christian armed forces. Even though the "Lebanese Forces" formally comprised several Christian organizations, the dominant and primary force in this organization, at the time under our scrutiny, was the Phalangists, led by the Jemayel family.

When the war broke out in Lebanon in June 1982, the Phalangist force included a nucleus of approximately 2,000 full-time recruited soldiers. In addition, the Phalangists had a reserve armed force—that is, men who served part-time in their free hours or when they were called up for special service. When fully mobilized, the number of Phalangist soldiers reached 5,000. Similarly, the Phalangists had militias in the villages. There were no ranks in this military force, but it was organized along military lines, with Bashir Jemayel as the military and political leader who enjoyed unimpeachable authority. The Phalangists had a general staff comprised of several commanders. At the head of this general staff was a commander named Fadi Frem; at the head of the Phalangists' intelligence division was a commander by the name of Elie Hobeika.

The link between the Christian forces and the State of Israel was formed shortly after the start of the civil war. In the course of time, this link grew stronger, from both political and military standpoints. The Christian forces were promised that if their existence were to become endangered, Israel would come to their aid. Israel extended significant aid to the Christian armed forces, supplying arms, uniforms, etc., and also training and instruction. Over the course of time, a considerable number of meetings were held between leaders of the Phalangists and representatives of the Government of Israel and the I.D.F. In the course of these meetings, the ties between the leaders of the two sides grew stonger. The Institute for Intelligence and Special Assignments (henceforth, the Mossad) was made responsible for the link with the Phalangists; and representatives of the Mossad maintained—at various times, and in various ways—a rather close connection with the Phalangist leadership. In the course of these meetings, the Phalangist leaders brought up various plans for strengthening the Christian forces' position, as well as various ways of bringing about the end of the civil war in Lebanon and restoring the independence of that nation, while [simultaneously] buttressing the status of the Phalangists and those allied with them in a regime that would be established in Lebanon. Israel's representatives expressed various reservations with regard to these plans and Israel's involvement in their realization.

A separate armed force is the military force in South Lebanon—the "Army of Free Lebanon" under the command of Major Haddad. This force comprises several hundred full-time soldiers. In addition, there is in South Lebanon a National Guard, which, under the command of local officers, does guard duty in the villages. Relations between the Phalangists and Haddad's men are not particularly close, for various reasons, and there were points of tension between these two forces. In 1982, soliders of both Major Haddad and the Phalangists wore uniforms provided by Israel—and similar to those worn by the I.D.F. The Phalangists' uniforms bore an emblem consisting of the inscription "Keta'ib Lubnaniyeh" and the drawing of a cedar, embroidered over the shirt pocket. Major Haddad's soldiers had an emblem on the epaulet inscribed with the words "Army of Free Lebanon" in Arabic and the drawing of a cedar. During the war, Haddad's force advanced and reached the Awali River. Pursuant to I.D.F. orders, Haddad's army did not proceed north of the Awali River.

The subject of the Palestinian population in Lebanon, from among whom the terrorist organizations sprang up and in the midst of whom their military infrastructure was entrenched, came up more than once in meetings between Phalangist leaders and Israeli representatives. The position of the Phalangist leaders, as reflected in various pronouncements of these leaders, was, in general, that no unified and independent Lebanese state could be established without a solution being found to the problem of the Palestinian refugees, who, according to the Phalangists' estimates, numbered half a million people. In the opinion of the

Phalangists, that number of refugees, for the most part Muslims, endangered [both] the demographic balance between the Christians and Muslims in Lebanon and (from other standpoints as well) the stability of the State of Lebanon and the status of the Christians in that country. Therefore, the Phalangist leaders proposed removing a large portion of the Palestinian refugees from Lebanese soil, whether by methods of persuasion or other means of pressure. They did not conceal their opinion that it would be necessary to resort to acts of violence in order to cause the exodus of many Palestinian refugees from Lebanon.

As we have said, the Mossad was the organization that actually handled the relations between the Phalangists and Israel, and its representatives maintained close contacts with the Phalangist leadership. In addition, the Intelligence branch of the I.D.F. (henceforth Military Intelligence) participated, albeit in a more limited capacity, in the contacts with the Phalangists; and it, by virtue of its job, was to issue a not insignificant number of evaluation papers on the Phalangists, their leaders, their aims, their fighting ability, etc. The division of labor between the Mossad and Military Intelligence with regard to the Phalangists, was spelled out in a document (Exhibit 189). While this division of duties left room for misunderstandings and also duplication in various areas, there is no room for doubt that both the Mossad and Military Intelligence specifically dealt with drawing up evaluations on the Phalangists, and each one of them was obligated to bring these evaluations to the attention of all interested parties. Neither the head of the Mossad nor the director of Military Intelligence disagreed with this in his testimony before us.

From the documents submitted to us and the testimony we heard, it emerges that there were differences of opinion between the Mossad and Military Intelligence with regard to the relations with the Phalangists. The Mossad, to a not inconsiderable extent under the influence of constant and close contact with the Phalangist elite, felt positively about strengthening relations with that organization, though not ignoring its faults and weaknesses. This approach of the Mossad came out clearly in the testimony we heard from the person who was in charge of the Mossad's contacts with the Phalangists. The head of the Mossad, in his testimony before us on 27.12.82, said, inter alia (p. 1437), that "the Mossad tried, to the best of its ability, throughout this period, to present and approach the subject as objectively as possible; but since it was in charge of the contacts, I accept as an assumption that subjective, and not only objective, relations also emerged. I must accept that in contacts, when you talk to people, relationships are formed." In contrast, Military Intelligence was to emphasize in its evaluations the danger in the link with the Phalangists, primarily because of this organization's lack of reliability, its military weakness, and other reasons we need not specify here. A characteristic expression of the difference in approach between these two agencies, whose responsibility it was to provide evaluations on the Phalangists and the desirability of relations with them, can be found in the exchange of documents when one of the intelligence officers (henceforth intelligence officer A, whose full name appears in the list of names in Section 1 of Appendix B) who served as a liaison officer on behalf of Military Intelligence in the Mossad's representation at Phalangist headquarters at the beginning of the war submitted an assessment (Exhibit 171) on cooperation with the Phalangists. This Military Intelligence officer rendered a negative evaluation, from Israel's standpoint, of the Phalangists' policy during the war and their aims for the future. This criticism was vigorously rejected by the Mossad (Exhibit 172).

The "Peace for the Galilee" war (henceforth the war) began on 6.6.82. On 12-14 June, I.D.F. forces took over the suburbs of Beirut and linked up with the Christian forces who controlled East Beirut. On 25 June the encirclement of West Beirut was completed and I.D.F. forces were in control of the Beirut-Damascus road. There followed a period of approximately one and a half months of negotiations on the evacuation of the terrorists and the Syrian forces from West Beirut, and during this time various targets in West Beirut were occasionally shelled and bombed by the I.D.F.'s Air Force and artillery. On 19.8.82 the negotiations on the evacuation of the terrorists and the Syrian forces from West Beirut were completed. On 23.8.82 Bashir Jemayel was elected president of Lebanon. His term of office was supposed to begin on 23 September 1982.

On 21-26 August, a multi-national force arrived in Beirut, and the evacuation of the terrorists and the Syrian forces began. The evacuation was completed on 1 September; however, according to information from various sources, the terrorists did not fulfill their obligation to evacuate all their forces from West Beirut and hand their weapons over to the Lebanese army but left in West Beirut, according to various estimates, approximately 2,000 fighters, as well as many arms caches, some of which were handed over by the terrorists to the Lebanese leftist militia "Mourabitoun." This militia numbered approximately 7,000 men in West Beirut, and it cooperated with the terrorists. After the evacuation was completed, the multi-national force left Lebanon (10-12 September 1982; cf. Section 2 of Appendix A for dates of stages of the war).

At the beginning of the war, the Chief of Staff [Lt.-Gen. Rafael Eitan] told the Phalangists that they should refrain from all fighting. This order was issued because of the fear that if the Phalangists' force got into trouble while fighting, the I.D.F. would be forced to come to its aid, thereby disrupting the I.D.F.'s plan of action. Even after I.D.F. forces reached the Damour-Shouf line, the I.D.F.'s orders were that the Phalangists would not participate in fighting (testimony of the Chief of Staff, pp. 195-6). After I.D.F. forces reached the area under Christian control, the Phalangist commanders suggested that a company of theirs of approximately 300 men set up a training base at a place called Beit Ad-Din, a site of historical importance in Lebanon. The Chief of Staff agreed to this, but made his agreement conditional on the Phalangist forces'exercising restraint and discipline, as the area was Druze. At first, this condition was honored; afterwards, there were outbursts of hostilities between the Phalangists and the Druze in Beit Ad-Din. The Druze committed some murders, and the Phalangists took revenge; a small I.D.F. force was stationed in the area in order to prevent such actions. In the early stages of the war there were also some acts of revenge and looting on the part of the Christians in Sidon; these were stopped by the I.D.F.

When I.D.F. forces were fighting in the suburbs of Beirut and along the Beirut-Damascus road, the Phalangists were asked to cooperate with the I.D.F.'s actions by identifying terrorists, a task at which the Phalangists'expertise was greater than that of the Israeli security forces. During these actions there were generally no acts of vengeance or violence against the Palestinian civilian population by the Phalangists who were operating with the I.D.F. Another action of the Phalangists' military force was the capture of the technical college in Reihan, a large building in Beirut, not located in a built-up area. The Phalangists captured this place from the armed Shi'ite organization "Amal." One day after the place was taken, the Phalangists turned the building over to the I.D.F. and left the site (testimony of the Chief of Staff, pp. 198-200).

The fighting actions of the Phalangists during that time were few, and in effect the fighting was all done by I.D.F. forces alone. This state of affairs aroused criticism and negative reactions from the Israeli public, and among I.D.F. soliders as well. This dissatisfaction was expressed in various ways; and in the political echelon, as well as in the media, there was amazement that the Phalangists were not participating in the fighting, even though the war was their battle as well, and it was only right that they should be taking part in it. The feeling among the Israeli public was that the I.D.F. was "pulling the chestnuts out of the fire" for the Phalangists. As the number of I.D.F. casualties mounted, public pressure for the Phalangists to participate in real fighting increased. The plan formulated in mid-June 1982, when it was still uncertain whether the terrorists would agree to leave West Beirut, was that the Christian forces would fight to take control of West Beirut; the I.D.F. would not take part in that operation; and only in the event that it became necessary would the I.D.F. help out the Phalangists with long-range artillery fire. This plan was discussed in the Cabinet meeting of 15.6.82, where it was proposed by the Prime Minister, and his proposal was adopted by the Cabinet, namely, that I.D.F. forces would not enter West Beirut, and this job was to be done by other forces (meaning the Phalangists) with help they would be given by the I.D.F. (transcript of the Cabinet meeting of 15.6.82, exhibit 53). Even after this resolution, no real fighting was done by the Phalangists for the purpose of extending control over West Beirut; and, as we have said, eventually the terrorists were evacuated as the result of a political agreement, after the I.D.F. had shelled various targets in West Beirut.

In all the testimony we have heard, there has been unanimity regarding [the fact] that the battle ethics of the Phalangists, from the standpoint of their attitude to noncombatants, differ greatly from those of the I.D.F. It has already been noted above that in the course of the civil war in Lebanon, many massacres had been perpetrated by the various forces that had taken part in the fighting. When the war began in June 1982, the prevailing opinion among the Mossad agents who had maintained contacts with the Phalangist leadership was that the atrocities and massacres were a thing of the past, and that the Phalangist forces had reached a stage of political and organizational maturity that would ensure that such actions would not repeat themselves. This opinion was based both on personal impressions of the character of the Phalangist leadership, as well as on the recognition that the interest of the Phalangist elite to eventually rule an independent Lebanese nation, half or more of whose population is Muslim and would be interested in maintaining relations with the Arab world, requires moderation of actions against Palestinians and restraint as to modes of operation. At the same time, there were various facts that were not compatible with this outlook. During the meetings that the heads of the Mossad held with Bashir Jemayel, they heard things from him that left no room for doubt that the intention of this Phalangist leader was to eliminate the Palestinian problem in Lebanon when he came to power—even if that meant resorting to aberrant methods against the Palestinians in Lebanon (testimony to pps. 16, 17, and 168 of the transcripts; Exhibit 85 of 30 June 1982, clause 14—Section 2 of Appendix B). Similar remarks were heard from other Phalangist leaders. Furthermore, certain actions of the Phalangists during the war indicated that there had been no fundamental change in their attitude toward different segments of the Lebanese population, such as Druze and Palestinians, whom the Phalangists considered enemies. There were reports of Phalangist massacres of women and children in Druze villages, as well as the liquidation of Palestinians carried out by the intelligence unit of Elie Hobeika (testimony no. 105 of intelligence officer B before the staff investigators, part of which appears in Section 3 of Appendix B; also, a document which mentions the Phalangist attitude toward terrorists they had taken prisoner—Section 4 of Appendix B, Exhibit 39). These reports reinforced the feeling among certain people—and especially among experienced intelligence officers—that in the event that the Phalangists had an opportunity to massacre Palestinians, they would take advantage of it.

The Assassination of Bashir Jemayel
and the I.D.F.'s Entry Into West Beirut
On Tuesday afternoon, 14.9.82, a large bomb exploded in a building in Ashrafiyeh, Beirut, where Bashir Jemayel was [meeting] with a group of commanders and other Phalangists. For the first few hours after the explosion, it was not clear what had happened to Bashir, and there were rumors that he had only been slightly wounded. Word of the attempt on his life reached the Prime Minister, the Defense Minister, the Chief of Staff, the director of Military Intelligence [Major General Yehoshua Saguy] and others in the early hours of the evening. During the evening, before it became clear what had befallen Bashir, the Defense Minister spoke with the Chief of Staff, the director of Military Intelligence, the head of the Mossad, and the head of the General Security Services about possible developments. He also spoke a number of times with the Prime Minister. Moreover, there were a number of conversations that evening between the Prime Minister and the Chief of Staff. Word of Bashir's death reached Israel at about 11:00 P.M., and it was then that the decision was taken—in conversations between the Prime Minister and the Minister of Defense and between the Prime Minister and the Chief of Staff—that the I.D.F. would enter West Beirut. In one of the consultations between the Minister of Defense and the Chief of Staff, there was mention of including the Phalangists in the entry into West Beirut. The question of including the Phalangists was not mentioned at that stage in conversations with the Prime Minister.

Once the decision was made to have the I.D.F. enter West Beirut, the appropriate operational orders were issued. Order Number 1 was issued at 12:20 A.M. on the night between 14.9.82 and 15.9.82. Orders Number 2 and 3 were issued on Wednesday, 15.9.82, and Order Number 4 was issued that same day at 2:00 P.M.; Order Number 5 was issued at 3:00 A.M. on 16.9.82; and Order Number 6 was issued on the morning of 16.9.82. The first five orders said nothing about entering the refugee camps, and only in Order Number 6 were the following things stated (Clause 2, Document no. 6, Exhibit 14):

"The refugee camps are not to be entered. Searching and mopping up the camps will be done by the Phalangists/Lebanese Army."

Clause 7 of the same order also states that the Lebanese Army "is entitled to enter any place in Beirut, according to its request."

Execution of the I.D.F.'s entry into West Beirut began during the early morning hours of 15.9.82.

On the night between 14.9.82 and 15.9.82, the Chief of Staff flew to Beirut with a number of people and met there with the G.O.C. Northern Command [Major General Amir Drori] and with the commander of the division (henceforth the division). Afterwards, the Chief of Staff, together with the people accompanying him, went to the Phalangists' headquarters, where, according to his testimony (p. 210), he ordered the Phalangist commanders to effect a general mobilization of all their forces, impose a general curfew on all the areas under their control, and be ready to take part in the fighting. The response of the Phalangist commanders who took part in that meeting was that they needed 24 hours to organize. The Chief of Staff requested that a Phalangist liaison officer come to the place where the division's forward command post was located (henceforth forward command post) under the command of Brigadier-General Amos Yaron. At that meeting, the Phalangist commanders were told by the Chief of Staff that the I.D.F. would not enter the refugee camps in West Beirut but that the fighting this entails would be undertaken by the Phalangists (Chief of Staff's testimony, p. 211). The Chief of Staff testified that the entry of the Phalangists into the refugee camps was agreed upon between the Minister of Defense and himself at 8:30 P.M. on the previous evening. The camps in question were Sabra and Shatilla. After the meeting in the Phalangists' camp, the Chief of Staff went to the forward command post.

The forward command post was located on the roof of a five-story building about 200 meters southwest of the Shatilla camp. The borders of the two camps were not defined exactly. The Sabra camp extended over an area of some 300 X 200 meters and Shatilla over an area of about 500 X 500 meters (testimony of the deputy assistant to the director of Military Intelligence, p. 29). The two camps were essentially residential neighborhoods containing, in the area entered by the Phalangists, as will be stated below, low permanent structures along narrow alleys and streets. From the roof of the forward command post it was possible to see the area of the camps generally, but—as all the witnesses who visited the roof of the command post stated, and these were a good number of witnesses whose word we consider reliable—it was impossible to see what was happening within the alleys in the camp from the roof of the command post, not even with the aid of the 20 X 120 binoculars that were on the command post roof.

It was not possible to obtain exact details on the civilian population in the refugee camps in Beirut. An estimate of the number of refugees in the four refugee camps in West Beirut (Burj el-Barajneh, Fakahani, Sabra, and Shatilla) is about 85,000 people. The war led to the flight of the population, but when the fighting subsided, a movement back to the camps began. According to an inexact estimate, in mid-September 1982 there were about 56,000 people in the Sabra camp (protocol, p. 29), but there is no assurance that this number reflects reality.

The Chief of Staff was in the forward command post from the early morning hours of Wednesday, 15.9.82. The I.D.F. began to enter West Beirut shortly after 6:00 A.M. During the first hours of the I.D.F. entry, there was no armed resistance to the I.D.F. forces, evidently because the armed forces that were in West Beirut were taken by surprise. Within a few hours, the I.D.F. forces encountered fire from armed forces that remained in a number of places in West Beirut, and combat operations began. The resistance caused delays in the I.D.F.'s taking over a number of points in the city and caused a change in the route of advance. In the course of this fighting three I.D.F. soldiers were killed and more than 100 were wounded. Heavy fire coming out of Shatilla was directed at one I.D.F. battalion (henceforth the battalion) advancing east of Shatilla. One of the battalion's soldiers was killed, 20 were injured, and the advance of the battalion in this direction was halted. Throughout Wednesday and to a lesser degree on Thursday and Friday (16-17.9.82), R.P.G. and light-weapons fire from the Sabra and Shatilla camps was directed at the forward command post and the battalion's forces nearby, and fire was returned by the I.D.F.'s forces.

On Wednesday, 15.9.82, the Minister of Defense arrived at the forward command post between 8:00 and 9:00 A.M. He met with the Chief of Staff there, and the latter reported on what had been agreed upon with the Phalangists, namely, a general mobilization, curfew, and the entry of the Phalangists into the camps. The Minister of Defense approved this agreement. From the roof of the command post, the Minister of Defense phoned the Prime Minister and informed him that there was no resistance in Beirut and that all the operations were going along well.

During the aforementioned meeting between the Minister of Defense and the Chief of Staff, present on the roof of the forward command post were the Defense Minister's aide, Mr. Avi Duda'i; the director of Military Intelligence, who came to this meeting together with the Minister of Defense; representative A of the Mossad (his full name appears in the list of names, Section 1, Appendix B); Major-General Drori; Brigadier-General Yaron; Intelligence officer B; the head of the General Security Services; Deputy Chief of Staff Major-General Moshe Levi; and other I.D.F. officers who were accompanying the Minister of Defense. Duda'i recorded in his notebook what was said and agreed upon at that meeting. According to Duda'i's testimony, he later copied these notes into another notebook, pages of which were presented before us (exhibit 103). These notes stated, inter alia, that the Phalangists were to be sent into the camps. The Minister of Defense spoke with the Prime Minister twice from the roof of the command post. According to the record of these conversations (Exhibits 100 and 101), in one of them the wording of the I.D.F. Spokesman's announcement was agreed upon as follows:

"Following the murder of President-elect Bashir Jemayel, I.D.F. forces entered West Beirut tonight to prevent possible grave occurences and to ensure quiet.

"The entry of the I.D.F. forces was executed without resistance."

From the forward command post the Minister of Defense went to the Phalangist headquarters. A record was made of this meeting, which was attended by a number of Phalangist commanders as well as the Minister of Defense, the director of Military Intelligence, the head of the General Security Services and representatives of the Mossad (Exhibit 79). At that meeting, the Minister of Defense stated, inter alia, that the I.D.F. would take over focal points and junctions in West Beirut, but that the Phalangist army would also have to enter West Beirut after the I.D.F. and that the Phalangist commanders should maintain contact with Major-General Drori, G.O.C. Northern Command, regarding the modes of operation. A record of this meeting was made by Intelligence officer B (Exhibit 28). From there the Minister of Defense went to Bikfaya, to the Jemayel family home, to pay a condolence call.

From the meeting with the Jemayel family in Bikfaya, the Minister of Defense went to the airport, and on the way he met with Major-General Drori at a gas station. This meeting took place in the presence of a number of people, including the director of Military Intelligence, the head of the General Security Services, Mr. Duda'i, and the bureau chief of the director of Military Intelligence, Lieutenant-Colonel Hevroni. The situation of the forces was discussed at this meeting, and Major-General Drori reported on the course of events during the I.D.F.'s entry into West Beirut. From there the Minister of Defense went on to the airport and met there with the Chief of Staff and the Deputy Chief of Staff at about 2:00 P.M., after which the Minister of Defense returned to Israel.

That same day, 15.9.82, while the Minister of Defense was in Beirut, a meeting took place at 11:30 A.M. in the Prime Minister's Office between the Prime Minister and others from the American embassy in Israel. During that meeting (protocol of the meeting, exhibit 120), the Prime Minister informed Mr. Draper that I.D.F. forces had entered West Beirut beginning in the morning hours, that there were no real clashes, that the I.D.F. action was undertaken in order to prevent certain possible events, and that we were concerned that there might be bloodshed even during the night. The Prime Minister also said that the Phalangists were behaving properly; their commander had not been injured in the assassination and was in control of his forces; he is a good man and we trust him not to cause any clashes, but there is no assurance regarding other forces. He added that the primary immediate task was to preserve quiet, for as long as quiet is maintained it will be possible to talk; otherwise there might have been pogroms, and the calm was preserved for the time being (Exhibit 120).

At 4:00 P.M. on Wednesday, 15.9.82, a briefing took place at the office of the Deputy Chief of Staff with the participation of the I.D.F. branch heads, including the assistant for research to the director of Military Intelligence. The meeting began with a review by the assistant for research to the director of Military Intelligence of possible political developments in Lebanon following the death of Bashir Jemayel. He stated, inter alia (page 4 of the transcript of the discussion, Exhibit 130), that the I.D.F.'s entry into West Beirut was perceived as vital not only by the Christians but also by the Muslims, who regarded the I.D.F. as the only factor that could prevent bloodshed in the area and protect the Sunni Muslims from the Phalangists. The Intelligence officer also stated that according to what was known to Military Intelligence, the attack on Bashir was carried out by the Mourabitoun, though that was not certain. During the meeting, the head of Operations Department announced that the Phalangists "are encouraging entry into the camps" (p. 7 of Exhibit 130). The Deputy Chief of Staff reported his impressions of the meeting at Phalangist headquarters in Beirut that day and said that the intention was to send the Phalangists into the refugee camps and afterwards perhaps into the city as well. He added that this "might create an uproar," because the armed forces in West Beirut that were then quiet might stir up a commotion upon learning that Phalangists are coming in behind the I.D.F. (page 11, Exhibit 130).

At 6:00 P.M. the Minister of Defense spoke with the Prime Minister from his home and reported (Exhibit 99) that by evening the I.D.F. would be in all the places; that he had conveyed the Prime Minister's words to Pierre Jemayel; and that "everything is in order" and the decision made on the previous night to send the I.D.F. into Beirut had been most important and [indeed] should not have been delayed.

The Chief of Staff remained at the forward command post in Beirut and followed the development of the I.D.F. actions from there. On that day the Phalangist officers did not arrive at the forward command post to coordinate operations, but Major-General Drori met with them in the evening and told them generally that their entry into the camps would be from the direction of Shatilla. Major-General Drori, who was not at ease with the plan to send the Phalangists into the camps, made an effort to persuade the commanders of the Lebanese Army that their forces should enter the camps and that they should prevail upon the Prime Minister of Lebanon to agree to this move. The reply of the Lebanese Army at the time was negative.

In the early morning hours of Thursday, 16.9.82, the Chief of Staff left the forward comand post and returned to Tel Aviv. That same morning, in the wake of political pressure, an order was issued by the Minister of Defense to halt the I.D.F.'s combat operations; but after a short time the Minister of Defense rescinded the order. At 10:00 A.M. the Minister of Defense held a consultation in his office with the Chief of Staff; the director of Military Intelligence, Brigadier-General Y. Saguy; Lieutenant-Colonel Zecharin, the Chief of Staff's bureau chief; and Mr. Duda'i (Exhibit 27 is a record of what was said at that meeting). The meeting was opened by the Chief of Staff, who announced that "the whole city is in our hands, complete quiet prevails now, the camps are closed and surrounded; the Phalangists are to go in at 11:00-12:00. Yesterday we spoke to them... The situation now is that the entire city is in our hands, the camps are all closed." Later on in his statement, while pointing to a map, the Chief of Staff stated that the areas marked on the map were in the hands of the I.D.F. and that the Fakahani, Sabra, and Shatilla camps were surrounded. He also said that if the Phalangists came to a coordinating session and wanted to go in, it was agreed with them that they would go in and that the Lebanese Army could also enter the city wherever it chose. At this discussion, the Minister of Defense spoke of the heavy American pressure to have the I.D.F. leave West Beirut and of the political pressure from other sources. In the course of the meeting, the Chief of Staff repeated a number of times that at that moment everything was quiet in West Beirut. As for going into the camps, the Minister of Defense stated that he would send the Phalangists into the refugee camps (p. 5, Exhibit 27). At the time of the consultation, the Minister of Defense informed the Prime Minister by phone that "the fighting has ended. The refugee camps are surrounded. The firing has stopped. We have not suffered any more casualties. Everything is calm and quiet. Sitting opposite me is the Chief of Staff, who has just come from there. All the key points are in our hands. Everything's over. I am bringing the Chief of Staff to the Cabinet meeting. That's the situation as of now..." After this conversation, the Chief of Staff reported on the contacts during the night of 14.9.82 with the members of the Mourabitoun, in which the members of this militia said that they were unable to hide, that they were Lebanese, and that they would undoubtedly all be killed by the Phalangists, whether immediately or some time later. The Chief of Staff added that "there's such a dual kind of situation that they're confused. They're seething with a feeling of revenge, and there might have been rivers of blood there. We won't go into the refugee camps" (p. 7, Exhibit 27). As stated, participating in this consultation was the director of Military Intelligence, who in the course of the discussion stated a number of things that appear in the aforementioned record.

The commanders of the Phalangists arrived for their first coordinating session regarding the entry of their forces into the camps at about 11:00 A.M. on Thursday, 16.9.82, and met with Major-General Drori at the headquarters of one of the divisions. It was agreed at that meeting that they would enter the camps and coordinate this action with Brigadier-General Yaron, commander of the division. This coordination between Brigadier-General Yaron and the Phalangist commanders would take place on Thursday afternoon at the forward command post. It was likewise agreed at that meeting that a company of 150 fighters from the Phalangist force would enter the camps and that they would do so from south to north and from west to east. Brigadier-General Yaron spoke with the Phalangists about the places where the terrorists were located in the camps and also warned them not to harm the civilian population. He had mentioned that, he stated, because he knew that the Phalangists' norms of conduct are not like those of the I.D.F. and he had had arguments with the Phalangists over this issue in the past. Brigadier-General Yaron set up lookout posts on the roof of the forward command post and on a nearby roof even though he knew that it was impossible to see very much of what was going on in the camps from these lookouts. An order was also issued regarding an additional precautionary measure whose purpose was to ascertain the actions of the Phalangist forces during their operation in the camps (this measure is cited in Section 5, Appendix B). It was also agreed that a Phalangist liaison officer with a communications set would be present at all times on the roof of the forward command post—in addition to the Mossad liaison officer at the Phalangist headquarters. The Phalangist unit that was supposed to enter the camps was an intelligence unit headed, as we have said, by Elie Hobeika. Hobeika did not go into the camps with his unit and was on the roof of the forward command post during the night (testimony of Brigadier-General Yaron, p. 726). This unit was assigned the task of entering the camps at that time for two reasons, first—since the . . . Phalangists had difficulty recruiting another appropriate force till then; second—since the members of this unit were considered specially trained in discovering terrorists, who tried to hide among the civilian population.

On 16.9.82, a document was issued by the Defense Minister's office, signed by the personal aide to the Defense Minister, Mr. Avi Duda'i, which contained "The Defense Minister's Summary of 15 September 1982." This document is (Exhibit 34) a summary of the things which Mr. Duda'i had recorded during his visit with the Defense Minister in Beirut on 15.9.82, as detailed above. In various paragraphs of the document there is mention of the Defense Minister's instructions regarding the entry into West Beirut. The instruction in paragraph F. is important to the matter at hand; it is stated there:

"F. Only one element, and that is the I.D.F., shall command the forces in the area. For the operation in the camps the Phalangists should be sent in."

The document is directed to the Chief of Staff, the Deputy Chief of Staff and the director of Military Intelligence. The document was received at the office of the director of Military Intelligence, according to the stamp appearing on the copy (Exhibit 35), on 17.9.82.

In the testimonies we have heard, different interpretations were given to the instruction that only the I.D.F. command the forces in the area. According to one interpretation, and this is the interpretation given the document by the Chief of Staff (p. 257), the meaning of the instruction is that in contacts with external elements, and especially with the Phalangists, only the I.D.F., and not another Israeli element, such as the Mossad, will command the forces in the area—but this does not mean that the Phalangist force will be under the command of the I.D.F. On the other hand, according to the interpretation given the document by the director of Military Intelligence (pp. 127, 1523), the meaning is that all forces operating in the area, including the Phalangists, will be under the authority of the I.D.F. and will act according to its instructions.

The entry of the Phalangists into the camps began at about 18:00 on Thursday, 16.9.82. At that time there were armed terrorist forces in the camps. We cannot establish the extent of these forces, but they possessed various types of arms, which they used—even before the entry of the Phalangists—against I.D.F. forces that had approached the area, as well as against the I.D.F. headquarters at the forward command post. It is possible to determine that this armed terrorist force had not been evacuated during the general evacuation, but had stayed in the camps for two purposes, which were—renewal of underground terrorist activity at a later period, and to protect the civilian population which had remained in the camps, keeping in mind that given the hostility prevailing between the various sects and organizations, a population without armed protection was in danger of massacre. It should be added here that during the negotiations for evacuation, a guarantee for the safety of the Muslims in West Beirut was given by the representative of the United States who conducted the negotiations, following assurances received from the government of Israel and from Lebanon.

Meanwhile, as we have said, the multi-national force left Lebanon, and all the previous plans regarding the control of West Beirut by the Lebanese government were disrupted due to the assassination of President-elect Bashir Jemayel.

**From the Entry of the Phalangists
into the Sabra and Shatilla camps
until Their Departure**

On Thursday, 16.9.82, at approximately 18.00 hours, members of the Phalangists entered the Shatilla camp from the west and south. They entered in two groups, and once they had passed the battery surrounding the camps their movements within the camps were not visible from the roof of the forward command post or from the observation sites on other roofs. The Divisional Intelligence Officer tried to follow their movements using binoculars which he shifted from place to place, but was unable to see their movements or their actions. With the entry of the Phalangists into the camps, the firing which had been coming from the camps changed direction; the shooting which had previously been directed against the I.D.F. now shifted in the direction of the Phalangists' liaison officer on the roof of the forward command post. G. (his full name appears in the list of names, Section 1, Appendix B) requested the I.D.F. to provide illumination for the force which was moving in, since its entry was taking place after dark. Initially, the illumination was provided by a mortar company, and subsequently also by aircraft; but because the illumination from the planes interfered with the evacuation of casualties of an I.D.F. unit, this source of illumination was halted;

mortar illumination continued intermittently throughout the night.

At approximately 8:00 P.M., the Phalangists' liaison officer, G., said that the Phalangists who had entered the camps had sustained casualties, and the casualties were evacuated from the camps. Major General Drori was at the forward command post from approximately 7:30 P.M. and followed the fighting as it was visible from the roof of the forward command post. He left the site after 8:00 P.M.

Several Intelligence Branch personnel, headed by the Division Intelligence Officer, were in the building on whose roof the forward command post was situated. The Intelligence Officer, who wanted to obtain information on the Phalangists' activities, ordered that two actions be carried out to obtain that information (these actions are detailed in Section 5, Appendix B). No information was obtained in the wake of the first action. As a result of the second action the Intelligence Officer received a report according to which the Phalangists' liaison officer had heard via radio from one of the Phalangists inside the camps that he was holding 45 people. That person asked what he should do with the people, and the liaison officer's reply was "Do the will of God," or words to that effect. The Intelligence Officer received this report at approximately 20:00 hours from the person on the roof who heard the conversation. He did not convey the report to anyone else, because an officers' briefing was scheduled to take place at field headquarters shortly afterward.

At about the same time or slightly earlier, at approximately 7:00 P.M., Lieutenant Elul, who was then serving as Chef de Bureau of the Divisional Commander, overheard another conversation that took place over the Phalangists' transmitter. According to Lt. Elul's testimony, while he was on the roof of the forward command post, next to the Phalangists' communications set, he heard a Phalangist officer from the force that had entered the camps tell Elie Hobeika (in Arabic) that there were 50 women and children, and what should he do. Elie Hobeika's reply over the radio was: "This is the last time you're going to ask me a question like that, you know exactly what to do"; and then raucous laughter broke out among the Phalangist personnel on the roof. Lieutenant Elul understood that what was involved was the murder of the women and children. According to his testimony, Brigadier General Yaron, who was also on the forward command post roof then, asked him what he had overheard on the radio; and after Lieutenant Elul told him the content of the conversation, Brigadier General Yaron went over to Hobeika and spoke with him in English for about five minutes (for Lt. Elul's testimony, see pp. 1209-1210a). Lt. Elul did not hear the conversation between Brigadier General Yaron and Hobeika.

Brigadier General Yaron, who was on the roof of the forward command post, received from Lt. Elul a report of what he had heard. According to Brigadier General Yaron's testimony, the report conveyed to him by Lt. Elul stated that one of the Phalangists had asked the commander what to do with 45 people, and the reply had been to do with them what God orders you to do (testimony of Brigadier General Yaron, pp. 696 and 730). According to Brigadier General Yaron, he understood from what he had heard that the reference was to 45 dead terrorists. In his testimony, Brigadier General Yaron linked this report with what he had heard in the update briefing that evening—which will be discussed below—from the Divisional Intelligence Officer. From Brigadier General Yaron's remarks in his testimony it emerges that he regarded the two reports—from Lt. Elul and from the Intelligence Officer—as being one report from two different sources. We have no doubt that in this instance there were two different and separate reports. As noted, the report which the Intelligence Officer obtained originated in a conversation held over the radio with Elie Hobeika. Although both reports referred to a group of 45-50 persons, and it is not to be ruled out that the questions asked over the radios referred to the same group of persons, it is clear, both from the fact that the replies given were different in content—the reply of the liaison officer was to do with the group of people as God commands, while Hobeika's reply was different—that two different conversations took place regarding the fate of the people who had fallen into the Phalangists' hands. As noted, Brigadier General Yaron did not deny in his testimony that Lt. Elul had translated for him and told him what he had heard when the two of them were on the roof of the forward command post. We have no reason to think that Lt. Elul did not inform Brigadier General Yaron of everything he had heard. It is noteworthy that Lt. Elul testified before us after Brigadier General Yaron had testified and before the notices were sent in accordance with section 15(A) of the law; and his statement to the Staff Investigators (no. 87) was also given after Brigadier General Yaron's testimony. Brigadier General Yaron did not testify again after the notice in accordance with section 15(A) had been sent, nor was there any request on his part to question Lt. Elul. We assert that Lt. Elul informed Brigadier General Yaron of the content of the conversation which took place with Elie Hobeika as specified above.

An additional report relating to the actions of the Phalangists in the camps vis-à-vis the civilians there came from the liaison officer G. of the Phalangists. When he entered the dining room in the forward command post building at approximately 8:00 P.M., that liaison officer told various people that about 300 persons had been killed by the Phalangists, among them also civilians. He stated this in the presence of many

23

I.D.F. officers who were there, including Brigadier General Yaron. We had different versions of the exact wording of this statement by Phalangist officer G., but from all the testimony we have heard it is clear that he said that as a result of the Phalangists' operations up to that time, 300 terrorists and civilians had been killed in the camps. Shortly thereafter, Phalangist officer G. returned to the dining room and amended his earlier report by reducing the number of casualties from 300 to 120.

At 20:40 hours that evening an update briefing was held in the forward command post building with the participation of various I.D.F. officers who were in the building at that time, headed by Brigadier General Yaron. The remarks made at that meeting were recorded by a Major from the History Section in the Operations Branch/Training Section. We were given the tape recording and a transcript thereof (Exhibit 155). At the meeting Brigadier General Yaron spoke of the I.D.F.'s progress and deployment, and about the Phalangists' entry into the camps and the combing operations they were carrying out. Following that briefing, the Divisional Intelligence Officer spoke. In the course of his intelligence survey regarding the terrorists and other armed forces in West Beirut, he said the following (pp. 4 and 5 of the transcript, Exhibit 155):

"The Phalangists went in today. I do not know what level of combat they are showing. It is difficult to see because it is dark... The impression is that their fighting is not too serious They have casualties, as you know—two wounded, one in the leg and one in the hand. The casualties were evacuated in one of their ambulances. And they, it turns out, are pondering what to do with the population they are finding inside. On the one hand, it seems, there are no terrorists there, in the camp; Sabra camp is empty. On the other hand, they have amassed women, children and apparently also old people, with whom they don't exactly know what to do (Amos, this refers back to our talk), and evidently they had some sort of decision in principle that they would concentrate them together, and lead them to some place outside the camps. On the other hand, I also heard from (the Phalangists' liaison officer, G.). . . that 'do what your heart tells you, because everything comes from God.' That is, I do not—"

At this time Brigadier General Yaron interrupted the Intelligence Officer and the following dialogue ensued between them:

Brigadier General Yaron: "Nothing, no, no. I went to see him up top and they have no problems at all."

24

Intelligence Officer: "People remaining in the field? Without their lives being in any danger?"

Brigadier General Yaron: "It will not, will not harm them."

Following this exchange, the Intelligence Officer went on to another subject. The Phalangists' actions against the people in the camps were not mentioned again in this update briefing.

In his testimony, Brigadier General Yaron explained his remark about his visit "with him up top and they have no problems at all" by saying that he had spoken several times that evening with the Phalangist officers on the roof of the forward command post after he had heard the first report about 45 people and also after the further report about 300 or 120 casualties; and even though he had been skeptical about the reliability of these reports and had not understood from them that children, women or civilians had been murdered in massacres perpetrated by the Phalangists, he had warned them several times not to harm civilians and had been assured that they would issue the appropriate orders to that effect (pp. 731-732).

Between approximately 22:00 hours and 23:00 hours the divisional Intelligence Officer contacted Northern Command, spoke with the Deputy Intelligence Officer there, asked if Northern Command had received any sort of report, was told in reply that there was no report, and told the Deputy Intelligence Officer of Northern Command about the Phalangist officer's report concerning 300 terrorists and civilians who had been killed, and about the amendment to that report whereby the number of those killed was only 120. The divisional Intelligence Officer asked the Deputy Intelligence Officer of Northern Command to look into the matter more thoroughly. Intelligence Officer A. was in the room while that conversation took place, and when he heard about that report he phoned Intelligence Branch Research at the General Staff, spoke with two Intelligence Branch officers there and told them that Phalangist personnel had so far liquidated 300 terrorists and civilians (testimony of Intelligence Officer A., p. 576). He went on to add that he had a heavy feeling about the significance of this report, that he regarded it as an important and highly sensitive report which would interest the senior responsible levels, and that this was the kind of report that would prove of interest to the director of Military Intelligence personally. In the wake of these remarks, the personnel in Intelligence Branch Research of the General Staff Branch who had been given the report carried out certain telephone clarifications, and the report was conveyed to various persons. The manner in which the report was conveyed and the way it was handled are described in Section 6, Appendix B. Suffice it to note here that a telephone report about this information was conveyed to Lt. Col. Hevroni, Chef de Bureau of the director of Military Intelligence, on 17.9.82 at 5:30 A.M. The text of the report, which was distributed to various Intelligence units and, as noted, also reached the office of the director of Military Intelligence, appears in Appendix A of Exhibit 29. That document contained a marking, noting that its origin lay with the forward command post of Northern Command, that it was received on 16.9.82 at 23.20 hours, and that the content of the report was as follows:

"*Preliminary* information conveyed by the commander of the local Phalangist force in the Shatilla refugee camp states that so far his men have liquidated about 300 people. This number includes terrorists and civilians."

The action taken in the wake of this report in the office of the director of Military Intelligence will be discussed in this report below.

On Thursday, 16.9.82, at 19:30 hours, the Cabinet convened for a session with the participation of—besides the Prime Minister and the Cabinet ministers (except for 5 ministers who were abroad)—a number of persons who are not Cabinet members, among them the Chief of Staff, the head of the Mossad and the director of Military Intelligence. The subject discussed at that meeting was the situation in Lebanon in wake of the assassination of Bashir Jemayel. At the start of the session, the Prime Minister reported on the chain of events following the report about the attempt on Bashir's life. The Minister of Defence then gave a detailed survey. The Chief of Staff provided details about the I.D.F.'s operation in West Beirut and about his meetings with Phalangist personnel. He said, inter alia, that he had informed the Phalangist commanders that their men would have to take part in the operation and go in where they were told, that early that evening they would begin to fight and would enter the extremity of Sabra, that the I.D.F. would ensure that they did not fail in their operation but I.D.F. soldiers would not enter the camps and would not fight together with the Phalangists, rather the Phalangists would go in there "with their own methods" (p. 16 of the minutes of the meeting, Exhibit 122). In his remarks the Chief of Staff explained that the camps were surrounded "by us," that the Phalangists would begin to operate that night in the camps, that we could give them orders whereas it was impossible to give orders to the Lebanese Army, and that the I.D.F. would be assisted by the Phalangists and perhaps also the Lebanese Army in collecting weapons. With respect to the consequences of Bashir's assassination, the Chief of Staff said that in the situation which had been created, two things could happen. One was that the entire power structure of the Phalangists would collapse, though as yet this had not occurred. Regarding the second possibility, the Chief of Staff said as follows (pp. 21-22 of Exhibit 122):

"A second thing that will happen—and it makes no difference whether we are there or not—is an eruption of revenge which, I do not know, I can imagine how it will begin, but I do not know how it will end. It will be between all of them, and neither the Americans nor anyone else will be of any help. We can cut it down, but today they already killed Druze there. What difference does it make who or what? They have already killed them, and one dead Druze is enough so that tomorrow four Christian children will be killed; they will find them slaughtered, just like what happened a month ago; and that is how it will begin, if we are not there—it will be an eruption the likes of which has never been seen; I can already see in their eyes what they are waiting for.

"Yesterday afternoon a group of Phalangist officers came, they were stunned, still stunned, and they still cannot conceive to themselves how their hope was destroyed in one blow, a hope for which they built and sacrificed so much; and now they have just one thing left to do, and that is revenge; and it will be terrible."

At this point the Chief of Staff was asked "if there is any chance of knowing who did it, and to direct them at whoever perpetrated the deed," and he continued:

"There is no such thing there. Among the Arabs revenge means that if someone kills someone from the tribe, then the whole tribe is guilty. A hundred years will go by, and there will still be someone killing someone else from the tribe from which someone had killed a hundred years earlier...

"I told Draper [U.S. ambassador] this today, and he said there is a Lebanese Army, and so on. I told him it was enough that during Bashir's funeral, Amin Jemayel, the brother, said 'revenge'; that is already enough. This is a war that no one will be able to stop. It might not happen tomorrow, but it will happen.

"It is enough that he uttered the word 'revenge' and the whole establishment is already sharpening knives..."

Toward the end of his remarks, the Chief of Staff referred to a map and explained that with the exception of one section everything was in the hands of the I.D.F., the I.D.F. was not entering the refugee camps, "and the Phalangists are this evening beginning to enter the area between Sabra and Fakahani" (p. 25). At that meeting the head of the Mossad also gave a briefing on the situation after the assassination of Bashir, but made no reference to the Phalangists' entry into the camps.

There was considerable discussion in that meeting about the danger of the United States at the I.D.F.'s entry into West Beirut, the general opinion being that the decision to go in was justified and correct. Toward the close of the meeting there was discussion regarding the wording of a resolution, and then Deputy Prime Minister D. Levy said that the problem was not the formulation of a resolution, but that the I.D.F.'s continued stay in Beirut was liable to generate an undesirable situation of massive pressure regarding its stay there. Minister Levy stated that he accepted the contention regarding the I.D.F.'s entry into Beirut, and he then continued (p. 91):

"We wanted to prevent chaos at a certain moment whose significance cannot be disregarded. When confusion exists which someone else could also have exploited, the situation can be explained in a convincing way. But that argument could be undercut and we could come out with no credibility when I hear that the Phalangists are already entering a certain neighborhood—and I know what the meaning of revenge is for them, what kind of slaughter. Then no one will believe we went in to create order there, and we will bear the blame. Therefore, I think that we are liable here to get into a situation in which we will be blamed, and our explanations will not stand up..."

No reaction was forthcoming from those present at the meeting to this part of Deputy Prime Minister D. Levy's remarks. Prior to the close of the session the Prime Minister put forward a draft resolution which, with certain changes, was accepted by all the ministers. That resolution opens with the words:

"In the wake of the assassination of the President-elect Bashir Jemayel, the I.D.F. has seized positions in West Beirut in order to forestall the danger of violence, bloodshed and chaos, as some 2,000 terrorists, equipped with modern and heavy weapons, have remained in Beirut, in flagrant violation of the evacuation agreement..."

Here we must note that the director of Military Intelligence was present at the outset of the meeting but left, after having received permission to do so from the Minister of Defense, not long after the start of the session, and certainly a considerable time before Minister D. Levy made the remarks quoted above.

Brigadier-General Yaron did not inform Major-General Drori of the reports which had reached him on Thursday evening regarding the actions of the Phalangists vis-à-vis non-combatants in the camps, and reports about aberrations did not reach Major-General Drori until Friday, 17.9.82, in the morning hours. On Friday morning Major-General Drori contacted Brigadier-General Yaron, received from him a report about various matters relating to the war, and heard from him that the Phalangists had sustained a number of casualties, but heard nothing about casualties among the civilian population in the camps (testimony of Major-General Drori, p. 404). That same morning Major-General Drori spoke with the Chief of Staff and heard from him that the Chief of Staff might come to Beirut that day.

In the early hours of that morning a note lay on a table in the Northern Command situation room in Aley. The note read as follows:

"During the night the Phalangists entered the Sabra and Shatilla refugee camps. Even though it was agreed that they would not harm civilians, they 'butchered.' They did not operate in orderly fashion but dispersed. They had casualties, including two killed. They will organize to operate in a more orderly manner—we will see to it that they are moved into the area."

Lieutenant-Colonel Idel, of the History Section in Operations Branch/ Training Section, saw this note on the table and copied it into a note-book in which he recorded details about certain events, as required by his position. It has not been clarified who wrote the note or what the origin was of the information it contained, even though on this matter the staff investigators questioned many persons who held various positions where the note was found. The note itself was not found, and we know its content only because Lieutenant-Colonel Idel recorded it in his notebook.

The G.O.C. held a staff meeting at 8:00 A.M. in which nothing was said about the existence of reports regarding the Phalangists' actions in the camps.

Already during the night between Thursday and Friday, the report about excesses committed by the Phalangists in the camps circulated among I.D.F. officers who were at the forward command post. Two Phalangists were killed that night during their operation in the camps. When the report about their casualties reached the Phalangists' liaison officer, G., along with a complaint from one of the Phalangist commanders in the field that the I.D.F. was not supplying sufficient illumination, the liaison officer asked Lieutenant-Colonel Treiber, one of the Operations Branch officers at the forward command post, to increase the illumination for the Phalangists. Lieutenant-Colonel Treiber's response was that the Phalangists had killed 300 people and he was not willing to provide them with illumination (testimony of Lieutenant Elul, pp. 1212-1213). Lieutenant-Colonel Treiber subsequently ordered that limited illumination be provided for the Phalangists.

In the early hours of the morning, additional officers at the forward command post heard from the Phalangists' liaison officer, G., that acts of killing had been committed in the camps but had been halted (statements 22 and 167).

At approximately 9:00 A.M. on Friday, Brigadier General Yaron met with representatives of the Phalangists at the forward command post and discussed wtih them the entry of an additional force of Phalangists into the camps. Afterwards, according to the testimony of Major General Drori (p. 1600), he met with Brigadier General Yaron in the *Cite* of Beirut, where they discussed the activity of the I.D.F. troops and other matters related to the war; but Brigadier General Yaron said nothing to him at that meeting about excesses committed by the Phalangists. Brigadier General Yaron's testimony contains a different version of the talk between him and Major General Drori that morning. According to that testimony, Brigadier General Yaron received reports that morning about a woman who claimed that she had been struck in the face by Phalangists, [and] about a child who had been kidnapped and whose father had complained to the Divisional Operations Officer; and Brigadier General Yaron had seen liaison officer G. arguing with other Phalangists. From all this Brigadier General Yaron inferred that something was amiss, or as he put it, "something smelled fishy to me" (p. 700). He phoned Major General Drori and told him something did not look right to him, and as a result of this conversation, Major General Drori arrived at the forward command post at approximately 11:00 A.M. According to Major General Drori, he arrived at the forward command post without having heard any report that something was wrong in the camps, simply as part of a routine visit to various divisions. We see no need to decide between these two versions.

When Major General Drori arrived at the divisional forward command post he spoke with Colonel Duvdevani and with Brigadier General Yaron. We also have differing versions regarding what Major General Drori heard on that occasion. In his statement (No. 2) Colonel Duvdevani related that he said he had a bad feeling about what was going on in the camps. According to his statement, this feeling was caused by the report of liaison officer G. about 100 dead and also because it was not known what the Phalangists were doing inside the camps. Colonel Duvdevani did not recall whether Major General Drori had asked him about the reasons for his bad feeling. Brigadier General Yaron testified (p. 701) that he had told Major General Drori everything he knew at that time, namely those matters detailed above which caused his bad feeling. According to Major General Drori's testimony, he heard about three specific matters on that occasion. The first was the blow to the woman's head; the second—which was not directly related to the camps—was that in one neighborhood, namely San Simon, Phalangists had beaten residents; and the third matter was that a feeling existed that the Phalangists were carrying out "an unclean mopping-up"—that is, their soldiers were not calling on the residents—as I.D.F. soldiers do—to come out before opening fire on a house which was to be "mopped up," but were "going into the house firing" (testimony of Major General Drori, pp. 408, 1593-1594). No evidence existed that, at that meeting or earlier, anyone had told Major General Drori about the reports of 45 people whose fate was sealed, or about the 300 killed; nor is there any clear evidence that he was told of a specific number of people who had been killed. After Major General Drori heard what he heard from Colonel Duvdevani and Brigadier General Yaron, he ordered Brigadier General Yaron to halt the operations of the Phalangists, meaning that the Phalangists should stop where they were in the camps and advance no further. Brigadier General Yaron testified that he suggested to Major General Drori to issue this order (p. 701). The order was conveyed to the Phalangist commanders. On that same occasion Major General Drori spoke with the Chief of Staff by phone about several matters relating to the situation in Beirut, told him that he thought the Phalangists had perhaps "gone too far" and that he had ordered their operation to be halted (p. 412). A similar version of this conversation appears in the Chief of Staff's testimony (pp. 232-233). The Chief of Staff testified that he had heard from Major General Drori that something was amiss in the Phalangists' actions. The Chief of Staff asked no questions, but told Major General Drori that he would come to Beirut that afternoon.

As mentioned above, the cable report (Exhibit 29) regarding 300 killed reached the office of the director of Military Intelligence on 17.-9.82 at 5:30 A.M. The text of this cable was transmitted to the director of Military Intelligence at his home in a morning report at 6:15 A.M., as part of a routine update transmitted to the director of Military Intelligence every morning by telephone. From the content of the cable, the director of Military Intelligence understood that the source of the report was Operations and not Intelligence, and that its source was the Northern Command forward command post. According to the testimony of the director of Military Intelligence, the details of which we shall treat later, he did not know then that it had been decided to send the Phalangists into the camps and that they were operating there; therefore, when he heard the report, he asked what the Phalangists were doing—and he was told that they had been operating in the camps since the previous day (pp. 120, 123). When the director of Military Intelligence arrived at his office at 8:00 A.M., he asked his bureau chief where the report had originated, and he was told that it was an "Operations" report. He ordered that it be immediately ascertained what was happening in the Sabra and Shatilla camps. The clarifications continued in different ways (described in Section 6 of Appendix B) during Friday morning, but no confirmation of the report was obtained; and the intelligence personnel who dealt with the clarifications treated it as a report which for them is unreliable, is unconfirmed, and therefore it would not be proper to circulate it according to the standard procedure, by which important and urgent intelligence reports are circulated. The content of the cable was circulated to a number of intelligence personnel (whose positions were noted on the cable form) and was conveyed to the Mossad and the General Security Services. Since the source of the report seemed to those Intelligence Branch personnel who dealt with the matter to be Operations, it was not accorded the standard treatment given reports from Intelligence sources, but rather the assumption was that Operations personnel were dealing with the report in their own way. The answers received by the director of Military Intelligence to his demand for clarification were that there were no further details. The director of Military Intelligence did not know that the report had been transmitted by Intelligence officer A. The report was transmitted verbally, incidentally, by the assistant to the bureau chief of the director of Military Intelligence to Lieutenant Colonel Gai of the Defense Ministry's situation room, when the latter arrived at about 7:30 A.M. at the office of the director of Military Intelligence. One of the disputed questions in this inquiry is whether Lieutenant Colonel Gai transmitted the report to Mr. Duda'i; we shall discuss this matter separately. Suffice it to say here that we have no evidence that the report was transmitted to the Defense Minister or came to his knowledge in another way.

At 7:30 A.M. on Friday there was a special morning briefing at the [office of] the assistant for research to the director of Military Intelligence. At the meeting, in which various intelligence personnel participated, the aforementioned report was discussed, and it was said that it can not be verified. The assistant for research to the director of Military Intelligence gave an order to continue checking the report. He knew that the source of the report was Intelligence officer A. The assistant for research to the director of Military Intelligence also treated this report with skepticism, both because the number of killed seemed exaggerated to him and since there had been no additional confirmation of the report (pp. 1110-1113). The director of Military Intelligence took no action on his part regarding the aforementioned report, except for requesting the clarification, and did not speak about it with the Chief of Staff or the Minister of Defense, even though he met with them that morning.

As mentioned above, the reports of unusual things occurring in the camps circulated among the officers at the forward command post already during the night and in the morning hours of Friday, and they reached other I.D.F. officers and soldiers in the area. At approximately

8:00 A.M., the journalist Mr. Ze'ev Schiff received a report from the General Staff in Tel Aviv, from a man whose name he has refused to disclose, that there was a slaughter in the camps. The transmitter of the report used the Arabic expression *dab'h*. He was not told of the extent of the slaughter. He tried to check the report with Military Intelligence and Operations, and also with the Mossad, but received no confirmation, except the comment that "there's something." At 11:00 A.M. Mr. Schiff met with Minister Zipori at the minister's office and spoke with him about the report he had received. Minister Zipori tried to contact the director of Military Intelligence and the head of the General Security Services by phone, but did not reach them. At approximately 11:15 A.M., he called the Foreign Minister, Mr. Yitzhak Shamir, and spoke with him about the report he had received from Mr. Schiff. According to the testimony of Minister Zipori, he said in that telephone conversation with Mr. Shamir that he had received reports that the Phalangists "are carrying out a slaughter" and asked that Minister Shamir check the matter with the people who would be with him momentarily and whose planned visit was known to Minister Zipori (Minister Zipori's testimony, p. 1097). According to Mr. Schiff's statement to the staff investigators (no. 83), Minister Zipori said in that conversation that "they are killing in the camps" and proposed that "it is worth checking the matter through your channels."

We heard a different version of the content of the conversation from Minister Shamir. Minister Shamir knew of the entry of the Phalangists into the camps from what he had heard at the aforementioned Cabinet meeting of 16.9.82. According to him, Minister Zipori told him in the aforementioned telephone conversation that he knows that Minister Shamir was to meet soon with representatives of the United States on the situation in West Beirut, and therefore he deems it appropriate to report what he had heard about what is occurring there. The situation in West Beirut is still not as quiet as it may seem from the media, and he had heard that three or four I.D.F. soldiers had been killed, and had also heard "about some rampage by the Phalangists" (p. 1232). Minister Shamir said in his testimony that as far as he could remember there was no mention in that conversation of the words massacre or slaughter. According to him, he was not asked by Minister Zipori to look into the matter, he did not think that he was talking about massacre, [rather] he got the impression from the conversation that its main aim was to inform him of the losses suffered by the I.D.F., and therefore he himself made no check and also did not instruct Foreign Ministry personnel to check the report, but asked someone in the Foreign Ministry whether new reports had arrived from Beirut and was satisfied with the answer that there is nothing new.

In addition, Minister Shamir thought, according to his testimony, that since a meeting would shortly be held at his office with Ambassador Draper, in which the Defense Minister, the director of Military Intelligence, the head of the General Security Services and their aides would be participating on the Israeli side, then he would hear from them about what was happening in West Beirut. This meeting was held at the Foreign Minister's office at 12:30, between Ambassador Draper and other representatives of the United States and a group of representatives of Israel, including the Minister of Defense, the director of Military Intelligence, and the head of the General Security Services (Exhibit 124). The Foreign Minister did not tell any of those who came to the meeting about the report he had received from Minister Zipori regarding the actions of the Phalangists, and he explained this inaction of his by the fact that the matter did not bother him, since it was clear to him that everything going on was known to the persons sitting with him, and he did not hear from them any special report from Beirut (p. 1238). The meeting ended at 3:00 P.M., and then the Foreign Minister left for his home and took no additional action following the aforementioned conversation with Minister Zipori.

Let us return to what occurred on that Friday in West Beirut.

In the morning hours, Brigadier General Yaron met with Phalangist commanders for coordination, and agreed with them that a larger Phalangist force would organize at the airport, that this force would not be sent into the camps until it receives approval from the Chief of Staff and after the Chief of Staff holds an additional meeting at Phalangist headquarters (pp. 705-706).

Already prior to the Chief of Staff's arrival, Major General Drori held a meeting with the commander of the Lebanese Army in which he again tried to persuade the commander, and through him the Prime Minister and Ambassador Draper, that the Lebanese Army enter the camps. Major General Drori told that commander, according to his testimony, the following (p. 1633):

"You know what the Lebanese are capable of doing to each other; when you go now to Wazzan [the Prime Minister of Lebanon] tell him again, and you see what is out here, and the time has come that maybe you'll do something, and you're going to Draper, to meet with Draper... get good advice from him this time, he should give it to you this time, he should agree that you enter the camps, it's important, the time has come for you to do it, and get good advice this time from Draper, or permission from him to enter or do it."

Major General Drori explained in his testimony that he had approached the commander so that the latter would speak with Ambassador Draper, since he had heard that Ambassador Draper had told the commander of the Lebanese Army a day earlier that the Americans would get the Israelis out of Beirut, that they should not talk to them and not negotiate with them. The answer which Major General Drori later received to his request from the commander of the Lebanese Army was negative.

On Friday, 17.9.82, already from the morning hours, a number of I.D.F. soldiers detected killing and violent actions against people from the refugee camps. We heard testimony from Lieutenant Grabowsky, a deputy commander of a tank company, who was in charge of a few tanks which stood on an earth embankment—a ramp—and on the adjacent road, some 200 meters from the first buildings of the camps. In the early morning hours he saw Phalangist soldiers taking men, women and children out of the area of the camps and leading them to the area of the stadium. Between 8:00 and 9:00 A.M. he saw two Phalangist soldiers hitting two young men. The soldiers led the men back into the camp, after a short time he heard a few shots and saw the two Phalangist soldiers coming out. At a later hour he went up the embankment with the tank and then saw that Phalangist soldiers had killed a group of five women and children. Lieutenant Grabowsky wanted to report the event by communications set to his superiors, but the tank crew told him that they had already heard a communications report to the battalion commander that civilians were being killed, [and] the battalion commander had replied, "We know, it's not to our liking, and don't interfere." Lieutenant Grabowsky saw another case in which a Phalangist killed a civilian. In the afternoon hours his soldiers spoke with a Phalangist who had arrived at the spot, and at the request of Grabowsky, who does not speak Arabic, one of the soldiers asked why they were killing civilians. The answer he received was that the pregnant women will give birth to terrorists and children will grow up to be terrorists. Grabowsky left the place at 16:00 hours. Late in the afternoon he related what he had seen to his commander in the tank battalion and to other officers. At their suggestion he related this to his brigade commander at 20:00 hours (Grabowsky testimony, pp. 380-388). In various statements made to the staff investigators, soldiers and officers from Lieutenant Grabowsky's unit and from other units stationed nearby related that they saw on Friday various acts of maltreatment by the Phalangist soldiers against men, women and children who were taken out of the camp, and heard complaints and stories regarding acts of killing carried out by the Phalangists. One of those questioned heard a communications report to the battalion commander about the Phalangists "running wild."

The battalion commander did not confirm in his statements (no. 21

and no. 175) and testimony that he had received reports on Friday from any of his battalion's soldiers about acts of killing or violent actions by the Phalangists against the residents of the camps. According to him, he indeed heard on Thursday night, when he was in the forward command post, about 300 killed, a number which was later reduced to 120 killed; but on Friday the only report he received was about the escape of a few dozen beaten or wounded persons northward and eastward, and this was in the afternoon. At a later date, after the massacre in the camps was publicized, the battalion commander made special efforts to obtain a monitoring report of the battalion's radio frequency and he submitted this report to us (Exhibit 1240). In this document no record was found of a report of acts of killing or maltreatment by the Phalangists on Friday.

We did not send a notice as per Section 15 to this battalion commander, and this for the reasons explained in the Introduction. We have not arrived at any findings or conclusions on the contradictory versions regarding the report to the battalion commander, and it appears to us that this subject can and should be investigated within the framework of the I.D.F., as we have proposed in the Introduction. For the purposes of the matters we are discussing, we determine that indeed I.D.F. soldiers who were near the embankment which surrounded the camp saw certain acts of killing and an attempt was made to report this to commanders of higher ranks; but this report did not reach Brigadier General Yaron or Major General Drori.

The Chief of Staff reached the airport at Khalde near Beirut at 15:30 hours with a number of I.D.F. officers. At the airport he met with Major General Drori and traveled with him to a meeting at Phalangist headquarters. Major General Drori testified that he had told the Chief of Staff on the way what he knew regarding the Phalangists' actions. The Chief of Staff was satisfied with what he had heard and did not ask about additional matters (Drori testimony, pp. 415, 416). Brigadier General Yaron joined those traveling to the meeting with the Phalangist commanders. The Chief of Staff testified in his first appearance that he had heard from Major General Drori and from Brigadier General Yaron only those things which he had heard on the telephone, and does not remember that he asked them how the improper behavior of the Phalangists had expressed itself. In that testimony he explained that he had refrained from asking additional questions since the discussion had dealt mainly with the situation in the city, that he generally does not like to talk while traveling, and that he thought the matter would be clarified at Phalangist headquarters, where they were headed (testimony of the Chief of Staff, pp. 234, 243). In his additional testimony before us, when the Chief of Staff was asked for his response to Major General

Drori's testimony that the latter had told the Chief of Staff about the three things which he knew about (see above), the Chief of Staff said that he is prepared to accept that these were the things said to him, but emphasized that the meaning of the things he had heard was not from his point of view that there had been acts of revenge and bloodshed by the Phalangists (p. 1663). In any case, according to his second testimony as well, the Chief of Staff was satisfied with hearing a short report from Major General Drori about the reasons for the halting of the Phalangists' actions, and did not pose questions regarding this.

At about 16:00 hours, the meeting between the Chief of Staff and the Phalangist staff was held. We have been presented with documents containing summaries from this meeting. In a summary made by Mossad representative A who was present at the meeting (Exhibit 80 A) it was said that the Chief of Staff "expressed his positive impression received from the statement by the Phalangist forces and their behavior in the field" and concluded that they "continue action, mopping up the empty camps south of Fakhani until tomorrow at 5:00 A.M., at which time they must stop their action due to American pressure. There is a chance that the Lebanese Army will enter instead of them." Other matters in this summary do not relate to the matter of the two camps (a summary with identical contents appears in Exhibit 37). We heard more precise details on the content of the meeting from witnesses who participated in it. The Chief of Staff testified that the Phalangists had reported that the operation had ended and that everything was alright, that the Americans are pressuring them to leave and they would leave by 5:00 A.M., and that they had carried out all the objectives. His reaction was "O.K., alright, you did the job."

According to the Chief of Staff, the discussion was very relaxed, and there was a very good impression that the Phalangists had carried out the mission they had been assigned or which they had taken upon themselves, and there was no feeling that something irregular had occurred or was about to occur in the camps. During the meeting they requested a tractor from the I.D.F. in order to demolish illegal structures; the Chief of Staff saw this as a positive action, since he had long heard of illegal Palestinian neighborhoods, and therefore he approved their request for tractors (pp. 234-239). In his second testimony, the Chief of Staff added that the commander of the Phalangists had said that there was almost no civilian population in the camps, and had reported on their killed and wounded (p. 1666). He did not ask them questions and did not debrief them about what had happened in the camps. They wanted to send more forces into the camps, but he did not approve this; and there was no discussion at that meeting of relieving forces (pp. 1667-1670). At the same meeting, the Chief of Staff approved the supply of certain arms to the Phalangists, but this has nothing to do with events in Beirut. Major General Drori testified during his first appearance that the commander of the Phalangist force, who was present at the meeting, gave details of where his forces were and reported heavy fighting—but did not make mention of any irregularities, and certainly not of a massacre. The Phalangist commanders spoke of American pressure [on them] to leave the camps. When Major General Drori was asked for additional details of that conversation he replied that he could not recall (pp. 415-420, 444). Brigadier General Yaron also testified that at that meeting the Phalangist commanders had said nothing about unusual actions in the camps, [that] the reason given for departure from the camps the next morning was American pressure, and that it seemed to him that the Chief of Staff even had had some good words to say, from a military standpoint, about their action. It was also agreed at that meeting that they would get tractors in order to raze illegal structures. At the end of the meeting it was clear to Brigadier General Yaron, as he testified, that the Phalangists could still enter the camps, bring in tractors, and do what they wanted—and that they would leave on Saturday morning (pp. 709-716).

In the matter of sending in additional Phalangist forces, Brigadier General Yaron testified that he did not think that limitations had been imposed on them with regard to bringing in an additional force, and he did not know whether they brought in an additional force after that meeting—but since they were supposed to leave at 5:00 A.M. on the following morning, there was no need for additional forces. On the same subject, Brigadier General Yaron also said that there was no restriction on the Phalangists' bringing in additional forces; it seemed to him that they had brought in a certain additional force—although the major force, at the airport, was not sent into the camps. He did not check whether they did or did not bring in additional forces, and from his point of view there was no impediment to their bringing in additional forces until Saturday morning (pp. 715-747).

Also present at that same meeting were the Deputy Chief of Staff, Mossad representative A, the divisional intelligence officer (who took the minutes of the meeting) and other Israeli officers; and there is no need to go into details here of their testimony on this matter, since the things they said generally agree with what has already been detailed above. We would add only that in the matter of the tractors, the Mossad representative recommended to the Chief of Staff that tractors be given to the Phalangists; but at the conclusion of the meeting, an order was given to supply them with just one tractor and to remove I.D.F. markings from the tractor. The one tractor supplied later was not used and was returned immediately by the Phalangists, who had their own tractors which they used in the camps that same night and the following morning.

It is clear from all the testimony that no explicit question was posed to the Phalangist commanders concerning the rumors or reports which had arrived until then regarding treatment of the civilian population in the camps. The Phalangist commanders, for their part, didn't "volunteer" any reports of this type, and this matter was therefore not discussed at all at that meeting. The subject of the Phalangists' conduct toward those present in the camps did not come up at all at that meeting, nor was there any criticism or warning on this matter.

During the evening, between 18:00-20:00 hours, Foreign Ministry personnel in Beirut and in Israel began receiving various reports from U.S. representatives that the Phalangists had been seen in the camps and that their presence was liable to lead to undesirable results—as well as complaints about actions by I.D.F. soldiers in the hospital building in Beirut. The Foreign Ministry personnel saw to the clarification of the complaints, and the charges against I.D.F. soldiers turned out to be unfounded.

After the Chief of Staff returned to Israel, he called the Defense Minister between 20:00-21:00 hours and spoke with him about his visit to Beirut. According to the Defense Minister's testimony, the Chief of Staff told him in that conversation that he had just returned from Beirut and that "in the course of the Phalangists' actions in the camps, the Christians had harmed the civilian population more than was expected." According to the Defense Minister, the Chief of Staff used the expression that the Lebanese Forces had "gone too far," and that therefore their activity had been stopped in the afternoon, the entry of additional forces had been prevented, and an order had been given to the Phalangists to remove their forces from the camps by 5:00 A.M. the following morning. The Defense Minister added that the Chief of Staff also mentioned that civilians had been killed (testimony of the Defense Minister, pp. 293-294). According to the Defense Minister's statements, this was the first report that reached him of irregular activity by the Phalangists in the refugee camps. The Chief of Staff did not confirm that he had told the Defense Minister all the above. According to him, he told the Defense Minister that the Phalangists had carried out their assignment, that they had stopped, and that they were under pressure from the Americans and would leave by 5:00 A.M.; and he does not recall that he mentioned disorderly behavior by the Phalangists, but he is sure he did not speak of a massacre, killing or the like. When the Chief of Staff was asked whether the Defense Minister had asked him questions in that same conversation, his reply was that he didn't remember (p. 243). In his second round of testimony, the Chief of Staff said that it was possible and also reasonable that he had told the Defense Minister the content of what he had heard from Major General Drori, although he reiterated that he didn't recall every word that was said in that same conversation (pp. 1687-1688). At the conclusion of his second round of testimony, the Chief of Staff denied that there had been discussion, in the telephone conversation with the Defense Minister, of killing beyond what had been expected (p. 1692).

This conversation was not recorded by anyone, and the two interlocutors testified about it from memory. It is our opinion that the Defense Minister's version of that same conversation is more accurate than the Chief of Staff's version. It is our determination that the Chief of Staff did tell the Defense Minister about the Phalangists' conduct, and that from his words the Defense Minister could have understood, and did understand, that the Phalangists had carried out killings of civilians in the camps. Our opinion finds confirmation in that, according to all the material which has been brought before us in evidence, the Defense Minister had not received any report of killings in the camps until that same telephone conversation; but after that conversation, the Defense Minister knew that killings had been carried out in the camps—as is clear from a later conversation between him and Mr. Ron Ben-Yishai, which we will discuss further on.

On Friday at approximately 4:00 P.M., when the television military correspondent Mr. Ron Ben-Yishai was at the airport in Beirut, he heard from several I.D.F. officers about killings in the camps. These officers were not speaking from personal knowledge, but rather according to what they had heard from others. Likewise, he saw Phalangist forces comprising about 500-600 men deployed at the airport. The Phalangist officer with whom Mr. Ben-Yishai spoke at that time told him that the Phalangist forces were going to the camps to fight the terrorists, so as to remove the terrorists and the arms caches in the camps. Asked what explanation had been given to the soldiers, the officer replied that it had been explained to them that they must behave properly and that they would harm their image if they didn't behave in the war like soldiers in all respects. He heard members of the forces in the field shouting condemnations and making threatening motions toward Palestinians, but he attached no importance to this, since he had encountered this phenomenon many times during the war. Mr. Ben-Yishai went from the airport to Ba'abda; and there, at 8:30 P.M., he heard from various officers that they had heard about people being executed by the Phalangists. At 23:30 hours, Mr. Ben-Yishai called up the Defense Minister and told him that a story was circulating that the Phalangists were doing unacceptable things in the camps. To the Defense Minister's questions, Mr. Ben-Yishai replied that he had heard this story from people he knew who had heard about civilians being killed by the Phalangists. The Defense Minister did not react to these words (statement 10 by Mr. Ben-Yishai, and testimony by the Defense Minister, p. 298). According to the Defense Minister, what he heard from Mr. Ron Ben-Yishai was nothing new to him, since he had already heard earlier about killings from the Chief of Staff; and he also knew that as a result of the report, entry by additional forces had been halted and an order had been given to the Phalangists to leave the camps (p. 298).

In concluding the description of the events of Thursday and Friday, it should be noted that no information on the reports which had arrived during those two days regarding the Phalangists' deeds, as these were detailed above, was given to the Prime Minister during those same two days. It should also be added that on Friday evening, there were several calls from U.S. representatives complaining about entry by Phalangist forces and about the consequences which might ensue, as well as about actions that had been taken in other parts of West Beirut. Foreign Ministry personnel handled these complaints, and a summary of them was also sent to the situation room at the Defense Ministry and was brought to the Defense Minister's attention at approximately 22:00 hours.

The Departure of the Phalangists
and the Reports of the Massacre
The Phalangists did not leave by 5:00 A.M. on Saturday, 18.9.82. Between 6:30-7:00 A.M., a group of Phalangist soldiers entered the Gaza Hospital, which is located at the end of the Sabra camp and which is run by the Palestinian Red Crescent organization. These soldiers took a group of doctors and nurses, foreign nationals working in that same hospital, out of the hospital and led them under armed escort via Sabra St. We heard from three members of the group, Drs. Ang and Morris and the nurse Ellen Siegel, about what happened in that hospital from the time of Bashir's murder until Saturday morning. As this group passed along Sabra St., the witnesses saw several corpses on both sides of the street, and groups of people sitting on both sides of the street with armed soldiers guarding them. The members of the group also saw bulldozers moving along Sabra St. and entering the camp's alleyways. The group of doctors and nurses arrived, with those who were leading

them, at a plaza at the end of Sabra St.; they passed by the Kuwaiti Embassy building and were brought into a former U.N. building by their guards. There several members of the group were interrogated by the Phalangists, but the interrogation was halted, their passports restored to them, and they were taken to a building where there were I.D.F. soldiers—that is, the forward command post. After a while, the members of the group were taken by I.D.F. soldiers to another part of Beirut, where they were released; and several of them, at their request, returned to the hospital after receiving from one of the I.D.F. officers a document which was meant to grant them passage as far as the hospital. We will return again later to the testimony of three of the members of this group.

When Brigadier General Yaron realized that the Phalangists had not left the camps by 06:30 hours, he gave the Phalangist commander on the scene an order that they must vacate the camps without delay. This order was obeyed, and the last of the Phalangist forces left the camps at approximately 8:00 A.M. Afterwards there was an "announcement"— that is, it was declared over the loudspeakers that people located in the area must come out and assemble in a certain place, and all those who came out were led to the stadium. There, refugees from the camps gathered, and the I.D.F. gave them food and water. In the meantime, reports circulated about the massacre in the camps, and many journalists and media personnel arrived in the area.

The Chief of Staff testified before us that on Saturday morning, the Prime Minister phoned him and told him that the Americans had called him and complained that the Phalangists had entered the Gaza Hospital and were killing patients, doctors, and staff workers there. The Chief of Staff's reply was that as far as he knew, there was no hospital called "Gaza" in the western part of the city, but he would look into the matter. At his order, an investigation was conducted in the Northern Command and also in the Operations Branch, and the reply he received was that there was indeed a hospital called "Gaza" but that no killings had been perpetrated, and he so informed the Prime Minister. According to the Chief of Staff's initial testimony, the Prime Minister called him on this matter at approximately 10:00 A.M. (p. 243). In his second round of testimony, when the Chief of Staff was presented with the fact that the Prime Minister was in synagogue at 10:00 A.M. on that same Saturday, the first day of the Rosh Hashana holiday, the Chief of Staff said that the first telephone conversation with the Prime Minister had apparently taken place at an earlier hour of the morning. The Prime Minister stated in his testimony that he had gone to synagogue at 8:15-8:30 hours, returning at 13:15-13:30 hours; that he had had no conversation with the

Chief of Staff before going to synagogue; that there had been no American call to him regarding the Gaza Hospital; and therefore, the conversations regarding the Gaza Hospital about which the Chief of Staff testified (pp. 771-772) had not taken place. The Defense Minister testified that the Chief of Staff apparently spoke with him by phone between 9:00-10:00 on Saturday morning and told him that the Prime Minister had called his attention to some occurrence at the Gaza Hospital; but the Defense Minister was not sure that such a conversation had indeed taken place, and said that he thinks that there was such a conversation (p. 300). We see no need, for the purpose of determining the facts in this investigation, to decide between the two contradictory versions regarding the conversations about Gaza Hospital. We assume that the contradictions are not deliberate, but stem from faulty memory, which is understandable in view of the dramatic turn of events taking place in those days.

On Saturday, the Defense Minister received additional reports about the acts of slaughter. He heard from the Director-General of the Foreign Ministry, Mr. Kimche, that Ambassador Draper had called him to say that I.D.F. soldiers had entered banks on the Street of Banks and that Palestinians had been massacred. It emerged that the report about the entry into the banks was incorrect. Regarding the report about the massacre, the Defense Minister's reply to the Foreign Ministry Director-General, which was given at about 13:00 hours, was that the Phalangists' operation had been stopped, the entry of additional forces blocked, and all the forces in the camps had been expelled. At 15:00 hours, Major General Drori spoke with the Defense Minister and told him about the reports concerning the massacre, adding that the Phalangists had already left the camps and that the Red Cross and the press were inside (testimony of Major Gen. Drori, pp. 428-429). At about 17:00 hours, Major General Drori met with a representative of the Lebanese Army and appealed to him to have the Lebanese Army enter the camps. The representative of the Lebanese Army replied that he had to get approval for such a move. Between 21:30 and 22:00 hours the reply was received that the Lebanese Army would enter the camps. Its entry into the camps was effected on Sunday, 19.9.82.

After the Phalangists had left the camps, Red Cross personnel and many journalists and other persons entered them; it then became apparent that in the camps, and particularly in Shatilla, civilians—including women and children—had been massacred. It was clear from the spectacle that presented itself that a considerable number of the killed had not been cut down in combat but had been murdered, and that no few acts of barbarism had also been perpetrated. These sights shocked those who

43

witnessed them; the reports were circulated by the media and spread throughout the world. Although for the most part the reports said that the massacre had been executed by members of the Phalangists, accusations were immediately hurled at the I.D.F. and at the State of Israel, since, according to the reports published at that time, the Phalangists' entry into the camps had been carried out with the aid and consent of the I.D.F. On Saturday and the days following, the I.D.F. refrained as far as possible from entering the camps, for fear that should any I.D.F. soldiers be seen there, accusations would be forthcoming about their participation in the massacre. The burial of the dead was carried out under the supervision of the Red Cross, and the victims' families also engaged in their burial.

It is impossible to determine precisely the number of persons who were slaughtered. The numbers cited in this regard are to a large degree tendentious and are not based on an exact count by persons whose reliability can be counted on. The low estimate came from sources connected with the Government of Lebanon or with the Lebanese Forces. The letter (Exhibit 153) of the head of the Red Cross delegation to the Minister of Defense stated that Red Cross representatives had counted 328 bodies. This figure, however, does not include all the bodies, since it is known that a number of families buried bodies on their own initiative without reporting their actions to the Red Cross. The forces who engaged in the operation removed bodies in trucks when they left Shatilla, and it is possible that more bodies are lying under the ruins in the camps or in graves that were dug by the assailants near the camps. The letter noted that the Red Cross also had a list of 359 persons who had disappeared in West Beirut between 18 August and 20 September, with most of the missing having disappeared from Sabra and Shatilla in mid-September. According to a document which reached us (Exhibit 151), the total number of victims whose bodies were found from 18.9.82 to 30.9.82 is 460. This figure includes the dead counted by the Lebanese Red Cross, the International Red Cross, the Lebanese Civil Defense, the medical corps of the Lebanese Army, and by relatives of the victims. According to this count, the 460 victims included 109 Lebanese and 328 Palestinians, along with Iranians, Syrians and members of other nationalities. According to the itemization of the bodies in this list, the great majority of the dead were males; as for women and children, there were 8 Lebanese women and 12 Lebanese children, and 7 Palestinian women and 8 Palestinian children. Reports from Palestinian sources speak of a far greater number of persons killed, sometimes even of thousands. With respect to the number of victims, it appears that we can rely neither on the numbers appearing in the document from Lebanese sources, nor on the numbers originating in Palestinian sources. A further difficulty in determining the number of victims stems from the fact that it is difficult to distinguish between victims of combat operations and victims of acts of slaughter. We cannot rule out the possibility that various reports included also victims of combat operations from the period antedating the assassination of Bashir. Taking into account the fact that Red Cross personnel counted no more than 328 bodies, it would appear that the number of victims of the massacre was not as high as a thousand, and certainly not thousands. According to I.D.F. intelligence sources, the number of victims of the massacre is between 700 and 800 (testimony of the director of Military Intelligence, pp. 139-140). This may well be the number most closely corresponding with reality. It is impossible to determine precisely when the acts of slaughter were perpetrated; evidently they commenced shortly after the Phalangists entered the camps and went on intermittently until close to their departure.

According to the testimony we heard, no report of the slaughter in the camps was made to the Prime Minister on Saturday, with the possible exception of the events in the Gaza Hospital, regarding which we made no finding. The Prime Minister heard about the massacre on a B.B.C. radio broadcast towards evening on Saturday. He immediately contacted the Chief of Staff and the Defense Minister, who informed him that the actions had been halted and that the Phalangists had been removed from the camps (p. 771).

When a public furor erupted in Israel and abroad in the wake of the reports about the massacre, and accusations were leveled that the I.D.F. and Haddad's men had taken part in the massacre, several communiques were issued by the I.D.F. and the Foreign Ministry which contained incorrect and imprecise statements about the events. These communiques asserted explicitly or implied that the Phalangists' entry into the camps had been carried out without the knowledge of—or coordination with—the I.D.F. The incorrect statements were subsequently amended, and it was stated publicly that the Phalangists' entry into the camps had been coordinated with the I.D.F. There is no doubt that the publication of incorrect and imprecise reports intensified the suspicions against Israel and caused it harm.

After the end of the Rosh Hashanah holy day, at 21:00 hours on Sunday, 19.9.82, a Cabinet meeting took place at the Prime Minister's residence with the participation of, in addition to the Cabinet members, the Chief of Staff, the head of the Mossad, the director of Military Intelligence, Major General Drori, and others. The subject discussed in that meeting was "the events in West Beirut—the murder of civilians in the Shatilla camp" (minutes of the meeting, Exhibit 121). At that meeting the Prime Minister, the Minister of Defense, the Chief of Staff, and Major General Drori reported on the course of events. The Defense Minister stressed that the I.D.F. had not entered the camps, which were terrorist bastions, because it was our interest not to endanger even one soldier in the camps (p. 5, minutes of the meeting). He added that on the day following the entry, "When we learned what had taken place there, the I.D.F. intervened immediately and removed those forces" (p. 6). According to him (p. 7) no one had imagined that the Phalangists would commit such acts. In his remarks, the Chief of Staff stressed, among other points, that in previous Cabinet meetings various ministers had asked why the Phalangists were not fighting—after all, this was their war. He, too, noted that no one could have known in advance how the Phalangists would behave, and in his view even the Phalangists' commanders did not know what would happen, but had lost control of their men. The Chief of Staff added that "the moment we learned how they were behaving there, we exerted all the pressure we could, we removed them from there and we expelled them from the entire sector" (pp. 9, 10). Major General Drori said that even before the Phalangists entered the camps, "We made them swear, not one oath but thousands, regarding their operation there. There was also their assurance that the kind of actions that were committed would not be committed. The moment it became clear to us what had happened, we halted the operation and demanded that they get out—and they got out." Major General Drori also told about the group of 15 persons, among them doctors, whom the I.D.F. had extricated from the hands of the Phalangists, thus preventing a major complication. He gave details of his appeal to the heads of the Lebanese Army that they agree to enter the camps, and about the negative replies he had received (pp. 18-22). Afterward the Chief of Staff spoke again, and according to the recorded minutes (p. 25) he said as follows:

"On Friday, I met with them at around noon, at their command post. We did not yet know what had happened there. In the morning we knew that they had killed civilians, so we ordered them to get out and we did not allow others to enter. But they did not say they had killed civilians, and they did not say how many civilians they had killed; they did not say anthing..."

In his second testimony the Chief of Staff explained that by his words, "In the morning we knew that they had killed civilians," he was referring to reports that existed on Saturday morning and not to the reports that existed Friday morning, as might have perhaps been understood (p. 1665). The remarks quoted above are not unequivocal; they are ambiguous. We accept the Chief of Staff's explanation that he was not referring to the reports in his possession on Friday, but to the reports that reached him on Saturday morning. This interpretation of the Chief of Staff's remarks is consistent with his other statements in this section of his remarks.

Several remarks were made in that meeting by the Prime Minister, who opened the session with a general survey in which he complained about accusations—in his view unfounded—which had been leveled against Israel. Various ministers took part in the discussion. In response to the remark of Minister Moda'i that the Prime Minister had spoken of "protecting life" as one of the goals of the entry into West Beirut, the Prime Minister stated (p. 73, Exhibit 12):

"That was our pure and genuine intention. That night I also spoke of this with the Chief of Staff. I told him that we must seize positions precisely to protect the Muslims from the vengeance of the Phalangists. I could assume that after the assassination of Bashir, their beloved leader, they would take revenge on the Muslims."

To this, Minister Hammer commented that "if we suspected that they would commit murder, we should have thought before we let them enter." The Prime Minister's reply was, "In the meantime days have passed. What are you objecting to? At night I said that we must prevent this." When in the course of his testimony the Prime Minister's attention was drawn to these remarks of his—that on the night when the decision about the entry into West Beirut was taken, he had spoken with the Chief of Staff about the goal "to protect the Muslims from the vengeance of the Phalangists"—he confirmed having said this, although he had not known at the time that the Phalangists would enter the camps (p. 764). In the Cabinet meeting of 19.9.82 the Chief of Staff did not react to these remarks by the Prime Minister, and did not deny them. In his second testimony the Chief of Staff said that in the conversation between him and the Prime Minister that night, the Prime Minister might have said "that there must be no rioting . . . they must not cross over or flee or not do things like . . . crossing from side to side"; but the Prime Minister had not gone into any greater detail (p. 1690). Since that night conversation was not taken down and it is difficult to rely on the memory of the conversants regarding the accuracy of what was said, we cannot determine with certainty what the Prime Minister said at that time, except for the fact that he mentioned that one of the purposes of the entry was to prevent rioting. The meeting concluded with a resolution to issue a communique expressing deep regret and pain at the injuries to a civilian population done by a Lebanese unit which had entered a refugee camp "at a place distant from an I.D.F. position." The resolution added that "immediately after learning about what had happened in the Shatilla camp, the I.D.F. had put a stop to the murder of innocent civilians and had forced the Lebanese unit to leave the camp." It was stressed in the resolution that the accusations regarding I.D.F. responsibility for the human tragedy in the Shatilla camp were in the nature of "a blood libel against the Jewish state and its Government," were groundless, and "the Government rejects them with repugnance." The resolution also stated that had it not been for the intervention of the I.D.F., the number of losses would have been far greater, and that it had been found that the terrorists had violated the evacuation agreement by leaving 2,000 terrorists and vast stocks of weapons in West Beirut. The resolution concludes:

"No one will preach to us moral values or respect for human life, on whose basis we were educated and will continue to educate generations of fighters in Israel."

The furor that erupted in the wake of the massacre, and various accusations that were leveled, led those concerned to carry out debriefings and clarifications. A clarification of this kind was carried out on behalf of the General Staff (Exhibit 239) and in the office of the director of Military Intelligence (Exhibit 29 from October 1982). The summation of the Military Intelligence report states that "it emerges from a retrospective examination that the telephone report . . . had its source in a rumor/'gut feeling' that the (Intelligence Officer A) had happened to overhear, and that he himself was unable to verify that rumor in his on-site examination, or in reaction to the briefings he had received..." The cable in question is Appendix A to Exhibit 29, which has already been quoted above; and from what has already been said above it is clear that it was not based on a "gut feeling." This investigative report contains other inaccuracies, which we shall note when we come to discuss the responsibility of Mr. A. Duda'i. A more detailed clarification was carried out in a Senior Command Meeting (SCM) with the participation of the Chief of Staff. The minutes of that meeting were submitted to us (Exhibit 241). At that meeting, the Chief of Staff said, inter alia, that whereas prior to the I.D.F.'s entry into Lebanon atrocities had been perpetrated throughout that country, after the I.D.F.'s entry "the Phalangists did not commit any excesses officially and did nothing that could have indicated any danger from them," and they looked to him to be a regular, disciplined army. In his remarks the Chief of Staff also stressed the pressure from various elements for the Phalangists to take part in the combat operations. Major General Drori related the course of events from his point of view, which in general lines is consistent with what he related in his testimony before us. He said, inter alia, that he had originally wanted the I.D.F. or the Lebanese Army to enter the camps, and that he did not concur in the considerations which had led to the decision regarding the entry of the Phalangists. Major General Drori was asked by one of the participants why a tractor had been needed, and he replied that there was a plan of the Lebanese administration, including the Phalangists and the Lebanese Army, to destroy all the illegal structures, including the many structures in the camps. Brigadier General Yaron also related the course of events. He said, inter alia, that when he had been informed by the command that approval had come to let the Christians into the refugee camp he had expressed no opposition or reservation, but had been quite pleased because it was clear to him that this camp contained many terrorists and the battalion had come under quite heavy fire from it. Brigadier General Yaron stressed that he had warned the Phalangists not to harm civilians, women, children, old people or anyone raising his hands, but to clean out the terrorists from the camps, with the civilians to go to the area of the stadium. He said that until Saturday morning he did not know what was happening and when he saw the group of doctors and nurses, they had not told him about the acts of slaughter either. Following a quite lengthy debate, Brigadier General Yaron responded to the remarks of the participants by stating, inter alia (pp. 85 to 87, Exhibit 241):

"The mistake, as I see it, the mistake is everyone's. The entire system showed insensitivity. I am speaking now of the military system. I am not speaking about the political system. The whole system manifested insensitivity...

"On this point everyone showed insensitivity, pure and simple. Nothing else. So you start asking me, what exactly did you feel in your gut on Friday . . . I did badly, I admit it. I did badly. I cannot, how is it possible that a divisional commander—and I think this applies to the Division Commander on up—how is it possible that a Division Commander is in the field and does not know that 300, 400, 500 or a thousand, I don't know how many, are being murdered here? If he's like that, let him go. How can such a thing be? But why didn't he know? Why was he oblivious? That's why he didn't know and that's why he didn't stop it . . . but I take myself to task...

"I admit here, from this rostrum, we were all insensitive, that's all."

At the conclusion of his remarks, the Chief of Staff stressed that if the I.D.F. had provided the Phalangists with the tank and artillery support they had requested, far more people would have been killed (p. 121).

On 28.9.82 a Senior Command Meeting was held with the Defense Minister, who related the course of events from his point of view. His remarks at that meeting are consistent with what we heard in his testimony. Several senior I.D.F. officers expressed their views at that meeting (Exhibit 242).

THE RESPONSIBILITY
FOR THE MASSACRE

In this section of the report, we shall deal with the issue of the responsibility for the massacre from two standpoints: first from the standpoint of direct responsibility—i.e., who actually perpetrated the massacre—and then we shall examine the problem of indirect responsibility, to the extent that this applies to Israel or those who acted on its behalf.

The Direct Responsibility

According to the above description of events, all the evidence indicates that the massacre was perpetrated by the Phalangists between the time they entered the camps on Thursday, 16.9.82, at 18:00 hours, and their departure from the camps on Saturday, 18.9.82, at approximately 8:00 A.M. The victims were found in those areas where the Phalangists were in military control during the aforementioned time period. No other military force aside from the Phalangists was seen by any one of the witnesses in the area of the camps where the massacre was carried out, or at the time of the entrance into or exit from this area. The camps were surrounded on all sides: on three sides by I.D.F. forces, and on the fourth side was a city line (that divided between East and West Beirut) that was under Phalangist control. Near the point of entry to the camps a Lebanese army force was encamped, and their men did not see any military force besides the Phalangist one enter the camps. It can be stated with certainty that no organized military force entered the camps at the aforementioned time besides the Phalangist forces.

As we have said, we heard testimony from two doctors and a nurse who worked in the Gaza Hospital, which was run by and for Palestinians. There is no cause to suspect that any of these witnesses have any special sympathy for Israel, and it is clear to us—both from their choosing that place of employment and from our impression of their appearance before us—that they sympathize with the Palestinians and desired to render service to Palestinians in need. From these witnesses' testimony as well it is clear that the armed military unit that took them out of the hospital on Saturday morning and brought them to the building that formerly belonged to the U.N. was a Phalangist unit. The witness Ms. Siegel did indeed tell of a visit to the hospital at 7:00 P.M. on Friday evening of two men dressed in civilian clothes who spoke to the staff in German, and she hinted at the possibility that perhaps they were Sephardic Jews; but this assumption has no basis in fact, and it can be explained by her tendentiousness. Ms. Siegel even said that these men looked like Arabs (pp. 499-500). It is clear that these men did not belong to an armed force that penetrated the camps at the time. The two doctors Ang and Morris did not see any other military force aside from the Phalangists, who presented themselves as soldiers of a Lebanese force. Dr. Ang also saw soldiers with a band with the letters M.P. in red on it. There is evidence that some of the Phalangist units who came to the camps wore tags with the letters M.P., and along the route the Phalangists traveled to the camps, road directions containing the letters M.P. were drawn. To be sure, Dr. Morris did not say specifically that the armed men who came to the hospital were Phalangists, but he described their uniforms, which bore Arabic inscriptions, and also heard them talking among themselves in Arabic and with someone from the hospital staff in French. Dr. Morris does not read Arabic, but Ms. Siegel, who does read Arabic, testified that the Arabic inscription was the one that signifies Phalangists. Therefore, the testimony of these three witnesses also indicates that the only military force seen in the area was a Phalangist one. A similar conclusion can be drawn from the statement of Norwegian journalist John Harbo (no. 62).

In the course of the events and also thereafter, rumors spread that personnel of Major Haddad were perpetrating a massacre or participating in a massacre. No basis was found for these rumors. The I.D.F. liaison officer with Major Haddad's forces testified that no unit of that force had crossed the Awali River that week. We have no reason to doubt that testimony. As we have already noted, the relations between the Phalangists and the forces of Major Haddad were poor, and friction existed between those two forces. For this reason, too, it is inconceivable that a force from Major Haddad's army took part in military operations of the Phalangists in the camps, nor was there any hint of such cooperation. Although three persons from southern Lebanon—two of them from the Civil Guard in southern Lebanon—were in West Beirut on Friday afternoon, and got caught in the exchanges of fire between an I.D.F. unit and Jumblatt's militia, with one of them being killed in those exchanges, this did not take place in the area of the camps; and the investigation that was carried out showed that the three of them had come to Beirut on a private visit. There is no indication in this event that Haddad's men were at the site where the massacre was perpetrated. We can therefore assert that no force under the command of Major Haddad took part in the Phalangists' operation in the camps, or took part in the massacre.

It cannot be ruled out that the rumors about the participation of Haddad's men in the massacre also had their origin in the fact that Major Haddad arrived at Beirut airport on Friday, 17.9.82. From the testimony of the I.D.F. liaison officer with Major Haddad's forces, and from Major Haddad's testimony, it is clear that this visit by Major Haddad to the suburbs of Beirut and the vicinity had no connection with the events that took place in the camps. Major Haddad arrived at Beirut airport in an air force helicopter at 8:30 A.M. on 17.9.82. The purpose of his visit was to pay a condolence call on the Jemayel family at Bikfaya. At the airport he was met by three vehicles with members of his escort party, who had arrived that morning from southern Lebanon. En route, they were joined by another jeep with three of Haddad's commanders, who also arrived to pay a condolence call. Major Haddad and his escorts paid their condolence visit at Bikfaya, and then for security reasons returned via a different route, arriving at the point where the road from Bikfaya meets the coastal road. From there, Major Haddad, along with about eight of his men, went to visit relatives of his in Jouniyeh. Following that visit to relatives, Major Haddad returned that same afternoon to his home in southern Lebanon, from where he phoned the aforementioned liaison officer that evening.

Hints were made about the participation of Haddad's men in the massacre on the basis of a southern Lebanese accent which several of the survivors mentioned, and they also said that a few of the participants in the massacre had Moslem names. This, too, does not constitute concrete evidence, since among the Phalangist forces there were also Shi'ites— albeit not many—and they were joined also by persons who had fled from southern Lebanon.

We cannot rule out the possibility—allthough no evidence to this effect was found either—that one of the men from Major Haddad's forces who was visiting in Beirut during the period infiltrated into the camps, particularly in the interim period between the departure of the Phalangists and the entry of the Lebanese Army, and committed illegal acts there; but if this did happen, no responsibility, either direct or indirect, is to be imputed to the commanders of Major Haddad's forces.

Here and there, hints, even accusations, were thrown out to the effect that I.D.F. soldiers were in the camps at the time the massacre was perpetrated. We have no doubt that these notions are completely groundless and constitute a baseless libel. One witness, Mr. Franklin Pierce Lamb, of the United States, informed us of the fact that on 22.9.82 a civilian I.D. card and a military dogtag belonging to a soldier named Benny Haim Ben Yosef, born on 9.7.61, were found in the Sabra camp. Following that testimony, these details were investigated and it was found that a soldier bearing that name was in a hospital after having undergone operations for wounds he sustained during the entry into West Beirut. A statement was taken from this soldier in Tel Hashomer Hospital. It emerged from his remarks that he is a soldier in the battalion, he arrived in Beirut on Wednesday, 15.9.82, his unit was moving not far from the Shatilla camp and was fired on; he was hit and the protective vest he was wearing began to burn. A medic cut the vest with scissors and threw it to the side of the road, as it contained grenades which were liable to explode. Personal documents belonging to the soldier were in the pocket of the vest. He was evacuated on a stretcher and taken by helicopter to Rambam Hospital. Already in the initial medical treatment his left arm was amputated; he was also wounded in the legs and in his upper left hip. It is clear that he was not in the camps at all. This testimony is confirmed by the statement of the medic Amir Hasharoni (statement 117). Evidently, someone who found the documents on the side of the road brought them to the camp, where they were discovered. The discovery of these documents belonging to an I.D.F. soldier in the camp does not indicate that any I.D.F. soldiers were in the camp while the massacre was being perpetrated.

Mr. Lamb also testified—not from personal knowledge but based on what he had heard from others—that cluster bombs were placed under bodies found in the camps, apparently as booby-traps. According to the witness, the I.D.F. used cluster bombs when the camps were shelled; these bombs explode easily and considerable caution is required in handling them, with only specially trained people having the technical knowledge to make use of these bombs as booby-traps. He raised the question whether the Phalangists, or the forces of Major Haddad—if any of them were in the camps—possessed the requisite technical skills to make use of these bombs as booby-traps. This question implies that the bombs were placed beneath the bodies by I.D.F. personnel. That implication is totally without foundation. As noted, Mr. Lamb had no personal knowledge regarding the use of such bombs as booby-traps, and it would be extremely far-fetched to view this section of Mr. Lamb's testimony as containing anything concrete pointing to direct involvement of anyone from the I.D.F. in the massacre that was perpetrated in the camps.

Following the massacre, the Phalangist commanders denied, in various interviews in the media, that they had perpetrated the massacre. On Sunday, 19.9.82, the Chief of Staff and Major General Drori met with the Phalangist commanders. Notes of that meeting were taken by a representative of the Mossad who was present (Exhibit 199). The Chief of Staff told the Phalangist commanders that he had come from the camps, it was said that a massacre had taken place there, and that for the sake of their future they must admit to having perpetrated the acts and explain the matter, otherwise they would have no future in Lebanon. Their reaction was that if the Chief of Staff says they must do so, they would. The Chief of Staff formed the impression that they were bewildered, that it was possible that they did not know what had happened in the camps and had no control over their people there (testimony of the Chief of Staff, p. 251). Even after that meeting the Phalangist heads continued in their public appearances to deny any connection with the massacre. That denial is patently incorrect.

Contentions and accusations were advanced that even if I.D.F. personnel had not shed the blood of the massacred, the entry of the Phalangists into the camps had been carried out with the prior knowledge that a massacre would be perpetrated there and with the intention that this should indeed take place; and therefore all those who had enabled the entry of the Phalangists into the camps should be regarded as accomplices to acts of slaughter and sharing in direct responsibility. These accusations too are unfounded. We have no doubt that no conspiracy or plot was entered into between anyone from the Israeli political echelon or from the military echelon in the I.D.F. and the Phalangists, with the aim of perpetrating atrocities in the camps. The decision to have the Phalangists enter the camps was taken with the aim of preventing further losses in the war in Lebanon; to accede to the pressure of public opinion in Israel, which was angry that the Phalangists, who were reaping the fruits of the war, were taking no part in it; and to take advantage of the Phalangists' professional service and their skills in identifying terrorists and in discovering arms caches. No intention existed on the part of any Israeli element to harm the non-combatant population in the camps. It is true that in the war in Lebanon, and particularly during the siege of West Beirut, the civilian population sustained losses, with old people, women and children among the casualties, but this was the result of belligerent actions which claim victims even among those who do not fight. Before they entered the camps and also afterward, the Phalangists requested I.D.F. support in the form of artillery fire and tanks, but this request was rejected by the Chief of Staff in order to prevent injuries to civilians. It is true that I.D.F. tank fire was directed at sources of fire within the camps, but this was in reaction to fire directed at the I.D.F. from inside the camps. We assert that in having the Phalangists enter the camps, no intention existed on the part of anyone who acted on behalf of Israel to harm the non-combatant population, and that the events that followed did not have the concurrence or assent of anyone from the political or civilian echelon who was active regarding the Phalangists' entry into the camps.

It was alleged that the atrocities being perpetrated in the camps were visible from the roof of the forward command post, that the fact that they were being committed was also discernible from the sounds emanating from the camps, and that the senior I.D.F. commanders who were on the roof of the forward command post for two days certainly saw or heard what was going on in the camps. We have already determined above that events in the camps, in the area where the Phalangists entered, were not visible from the roof of the forward command post. It has also been made clear that no sounds from which it could be inferred that a massacre was being perpetrated in the camps reached that place. It is true that certain reports did reach officers at the forward command post—and we shall discuss these in another section of this report—but from the roof of the forward command post they neither saw the actions of the Phalangists nor heard any sounds indicating that a massacre was in progress.

Here we must add that when the group of doctors and nurses met I.D.F. officers on Saturday morning, at a time when it was already clear to them that they were out of danger, they made no complaint that a massacre had been perpetrated in the camps. When we asked the witnesses from the group why they had not informed the I.D.F. officers about the massacre, they replied that they had not known about it. The fact that the doctors and nurses who were in the Gaza Hospital—which is proximate to the site of the event and where persons wounded in combative action and frightened persons from the camps arrived—did not know about the massacre, but only about isolated instances of injury which they had seen for themselves, also shows that those who were nearby but not actually inside the camps did not form the impression, from what they saw and heard, that a massacre of hundreds of people was taking place. Nor did members of a unit of the Lebanese Army who were stationed near the places of entry into the camps know anything about the massacre until after the Phalangists had departed.

Our conclusion is therefore that the direct responsibility for the perpetration of the acts of slaughter rests on the Phalangist forces. No evidence was brought before us that Phalangist personnel received explicit orders from their command to perpetrate acts of slaughter, but it is evident that the forces who entered the area were steeped in hatred for the Palestinians, in the wake of the atrocities and severe injuries done to the Christians during the civil war in Lebanon by the Palestinians and those who fought alongside them; and these feelings of hatred were compounded by a longing for revenge in the wake of the assassination of the Phalangists' admired leader, Bashir, and the killing of several dozen Phalangists two days before their entry into the camps. The execution of acts of slaughter was approved for the Phalangists on the site by the remarks of the two commanders to whom questions were addressed over the radios, as was related above.

The Indirect Responsibility

Before we discuss the essence of the problem of the indirect responsibility of Israel, or of those who operated at its behest, we perceive it to be necessary to deal with objections that have been voiced on various occasions, according to which if Israel's direct responsibility for the atrocities is negated—i.e., if it is determined that the blood of those killed was not shed by I.D.F. soldiers and I.D.F. forces, or that others operating at the behest of the state were not parties to the atrocities— then there is no place for further discussion of the problem of indirect responsibility. The argument is that no responsibility should be laid on Israel for deeds perpetrated outside of its borders by members of the Christian community against Palestinians in that same country, or against Muslims located within the area of the camps. A certain echo of this approach may be found in statements made in the Cabinet meeting of 19.9.82, and in statements released to the public by various sources.

We cannot accept this position. If it indeed becomes clear that those who decided on the entry of the Phalangists into the camps should have foreseen—from the information at their disposal and from things which were common knowledge—that there was danger of a massacre, and no steps were taken which might have prevented this danger or at least greatly reduced the possibility that deeds of this type might be done, then those who made the decisions and those who implemented them are indirectly responsible for what ultimately occurred, even if they did not intend this to happen and merely disregarded the anticipated danger. A similar indirect responsibility also falls on those who knew of the decision: it was their duty, by virtue of their position and their office, to warn of the danger, and they did not fulfill this duty. It is also not possible to absolve of such indirect responsibility those persons who, when they received the first reports of what was happening in the camps, did not rush to prevent the continuation of the Phalangists' actions and did not do everything within their power to stop them. It is not our function as a commission of inquiry to lay a precise legal foundation for such indirect responsibility. It may be that from a legal perspective, the issue of responsibility is not unequivocal, in view of the lack of clarity regarding the status of the State of Israel and its forces in Lebanese territory. If the territory of West Beirut may be viewed at the time of the events as occupied territory—and we do not determine that such indeed is the case from a legal perspective—then it is the duty of the occupier, according to the rules of usual and customary international law, to do all it can to ensure the public's well-being and security. Even if these legal norms are invalid regarding the situation in which the Israeli government and the forces operating at its instructions found themselves at the time of the events, still, as far as the obligations applying to every civilized nation and the ethical rules accepted by civilized peoples go, the problem of indirect responsibility cannot be disregarded. A basis for such responsibility may be found in the outlook of our ancestors, which was expressed in things that were said about the moral significance of the biblical portion concerning the "beheaded heifer" (in the Book of Deuteronomy, chapter 21). It is said in Deuteronomy (21:6-7) that the elders of the city who were near the slain victim who has been found (and it is not known who struck him down) "will wash their hands over the beheaded heifer in the valley and reply: our hands did not shed this blood and our eyes did not see." Rabbi Yehoshua ben Levi says of this verse (Talmud, Tractate Sota 38b):

"The necessity for the heifer whose neck is to be broken only arises on account of the niggardliness of spirit, as it is said, 'Our hands have not shed this blood.' But can it enter our minds that the elders of a Court of Justice are shedders of blood! The meaning is, [the man found dead] did not come to us for help and we dismissed him, we did not see him and let him go—i.e., he did not come to us for help and we dismissed him without supplying him with food, we did not see him and let him go without escort." (Rashi explains that escort means a group that would accompany them; Sforno, a commentator from a later period, says in his commentary on Deuteronomy, "that there should not be spectators at the place, for if there were spectators there, they would protest and speak out.")

When we are dealing with the issue of indirect responsibility, it should also not be forgotten that the Jews in various lands of exile, and also in the Land of Israel when it was under foreign rule, suffered greatly from pogroms perpetrated by various hooligans; and the danger of disturbances against Jews in various lands, it seems evident, has not yet passed. The Jewish public's stand has always been that the responsibility for such deeds falls not only on those who rioted and committed the atrocities, but also on those who were responsible for safety and public order, who could have prevented the disturbances and did not fulfill their obligations in this respect. It is true that the regimes of various countries, among them even enlightened countries, have side-stepped such responsibility on more than one occasion and have not established inquiry commissions to investigate the issue of indirect responsibility, such as that about which we are speaking; but the development of ethical norms in the world public requires that the approach to this issue be universally shared, and that the responsibility be placed not just on the perpetrators, but also on those who could and should have prevented the commission of those deeds which must be condemned.

We would like to note here that we will not enter at all into the question of indirect responsibility of other elements besides the State of Israel. One might argue that such indirect responsibility falls, inter alia, on the Lebanese Army, or on the Lebanese government to whose orders this army was subject, since despite Major General Drori's urgings in his talks with the heads of the Lebanese Army, they did not grant Israel's request to enter the camps before the Phalangists or instead of the Phalangists, until 19.9.82. It should also be noted that in meetings with U.S. representatives during the critical days, Israel's spokesmen repeatedly requested that the U.S. use its influence to get the Lebanese Army to fulfill the function of maintaining public peace and order in West Beirut, but it does not seem that these requests had any result. One might also make charges concerning the hasty evacuation of the multi-national force by the countries whose troops were in place until after the evacuation of the terrorists. We will also not discuss the question of when other elements besides Israeli elements first learned of the massacre, and whether they did all they could to stop it or at least to immediately bring the reports in their possession to Israeli and other elements. We do not view it as our function to discuss these issues, which perhaps should be clarified in another framework; we will only discuss the issue of Israel's indirect responsibility, knowing that if this responsibility is determined, it is not an exclusive responsibility laid on Israel alone.

Here it is appropriate to discuss the question of whether blame may be attached regarding the atrocities done in the camps to those who decided on the entry into West Beirut and on including the Phalangists in actions linked to this entry.

As has already been said above, the decision to enter West Beirut was adopted in conversations held between the Prime Minister and the Defense Minister on the night between 14-15 September 1982. No charge may be made against this decision for having been adopted by these two alone without convening a Cabinet session. On that same night, an extraordinary emergency situation was created which justified immediate and concerted action to prevent a situation which appeared undesirable and even dangerous from Isreal's perspective. There is great sense in the supposition that had I.D.F. troops not entered West Beirut, a situation of total chaos and battles between various combat forces would have developed, and the number of victims among the civilian population would have been far greater than it ultimately was. The Israeli military force was the only real force nearby which could take control over West

Beirut so as to maintain the peace and prevent a resumption of hostile actions between various militias and communities. The Lebanese Army could have performed a function in the refugee camps, but it did not then have the power to enforce order in all of West Beirut. Under these circumstances it could be assumed that were I.D.F. forces not to enter West Beirut, various atrocities would be perpetrated there in the absence of any real authority; and it may be that world public opinion might then have placed responsibility on Israel for having refrained from action.

Both the Prime Minister and the Defense Minister based the participation of the Phalangists in the entry into West Beirut on the Cabinet resolution adopted at the session of 15.6.82. We are unable to accept this reasoning. Although there was much talk in the meeting of 15.6.82 (Exhibit 53) about the plan that the I.D.F. would not enter West Beirut, and that the entry would be effected by the Phalangists with support from the I.D.F.—but the situation then was wholly different from the one that emerged subsequently. During the discussion of 15.6.82 the terrorists and Syrian forces had not yet been evacuated from West Beirut, and the entire military picture was different from the one that developed after the evacuation was executed and after Bashir's assassination. However, even if the Phalangists' participation was not based on a formal Cabinet resolution of 15.6.82, we found no cause to raise objections to that participation in the circumstances that were created after Bashir's assassination. We wish to stress that we are speaking now only of the Phalangists' participation in connection with the entry into West Beirut, and not about the role they were to play in the camps.

The demand made in Israel to have the Phalangists take part in the fighting was a general and understandable one; and political, and to some extent military, reasons existed for such participation. The general question of relations with the Phalangists and cooperation with them is a saliently political one, regarding which there may be legitimate differences of opinion and outlook. We do not find it justified to assert that the decision on this participation was unwarranted or that it should not have been made.

It is a different question whether the decision to have the Phalangists enter the camps was justified in the circumstances that were created. From the description of events cited above and from the testimony before us, it is clear that this decision was taken by the Minister of Defense with the concurrence of the Chief of Staff and that the Prime Minister did not know of it until the Cabinet session in the evening hours of 16.9.82. We shall leave to another section of this report—which will deal with the personal responsibility of all those to whom notices were sent under Section 15(A) of the law—the discussion of whether personal responsibility devolves upon the Defense Minister or the Chief of Staff for what happened afterward in the camps in the wake of the decision to have the Phalangists enter them. Here we shall discuss only the question of whether it was possible or necessary to foresee that the entry of the Phalangists into the camps, with them in control of the area where the Palestinian population was to be found, was liable to eventuate in a massacre, as in fact finally happened.

The heads of Government in Israel and the heads of the I.D.F. who testified before us were for the most part firm in their view that what happened in the camps was an unexpected occurrence, in the nature of a disaster which no one had imagined and which could not have been—or, at all events, need not have been—foreseen. It was stressed in the remarks made in testimony and in the arguments advanced before us, that this matter should not be discussed in terms of hindsight, but that we must be careful to judge without taking into account what actually happened. We concur that special caution is required so as not to fall into the hindsight trap, but that caution does not exempt us from the obligation to examine whether persons acting and thinking rationally were duty-bound, when the decision was taken to have the Phalangists enter the camps, to foresee, according to the information that each of them possessed and according to public knowledge, that the entry of the Phalangists into the camps held out the danger of a massacre and that no little probability existed that it would in fact occur. At this stage of the discussion we shall not pause to examine the particular information possessed by the persons to whom notices were sent under Section 15(A) of the law, but shall make do with an examination of the knowledge possessed by everyone who had some expertise on the subject of Lebanon.

In our view, everyone who had anything to do with events in Lebanon should have felt apprehension about a massacre in the camps, if armed Phalangist forces were to be moved into them without the I.D.F. exercising concrete and effective supervision and scrutiny of them. All those concerned were well aware that combat morality among the various combatant groups in Lebanon differs from the norm in the I.D.F., that the combatants in Lebanon belittle the value of human life far beyond what is necessary and accepted in wars between civilized peoples, and that various atrocities against the noncombatant population had been widespread in Lebanon since 1975. It was well known that the Phalangists harbor deep enmity for the Palestinians, viewing them as the source of all the troubles that afflicted Lebanon during the years of the civil war. The fact that in certain operations carried out under close I.D.F. supervision the Phalangists did not deviate from disciplined behavior could not serve as an indication that their attitude toward the Palestinian population had changed, or that changes had been effected in their plans—which they made no effort to hide—for the Palestinians. To this backdrop of the Phalangists' attitude toward the Palestinians were added the profound shock in the wake of Bashir's death along with a group of Phalangists in the explosion at Ashrafiya, and the feeling of revenge that event must arouse, even without the identity of the assailant being known.

The written and oral summations presented to us stressed that most of the experts whose remarks were brought before the commission—both Military Intelligence personnel and Mossad personnel—had expressed the view that given the state of affairs existing when the decision was taken to have the Phalangists enter the camps, it could not be foreseen that the Phalangists would perpetrate a massacre, or at all events the probability of that occurring was low; and had they been asked for their opinion at the time they would have raised no objections to the decision. We are not prepared to attach any importance to these statements, and not necessarily due to the fact that this evaluation was refuted by reality. It is our impression that the remarks of the experts on this matter were influenced to a certain extent by the desire of each of them to justify his action or lack thereof, the experts having failed to raise any objection to the entry of the Phalangists into the camps when they learned of it. In contrast to the approach of these experts, there were cases in which other personnel, both from Military Intelligence, from other I.D.F. branches, and from outside the governmental framework, warned—as soon as they learned of the Phalangists' entry into the camps, and on earlier occasions when the Phalangists' role in the war was discussed— that the danger of a massacre was great and that the Phalangists would take advantage of every opportunity offered them to wreak vengeance on the Palestinians. Thus, for example, Intelligence Officer G. (whose name appears in Section 1 of Appendix B), a branch head in Military Intelligence/Research, stated that the subject of possible injury by the Phalangists to the Palestinian population had come up many times in internal discussions (statement no. 176). Similarly, when Intelligence Officer A. learned on Thursday, in a briefing of Intelligence officers, that the Phalangists had entered the camps, he said, even before the report arrived about the 300 killed, that he was convinced that the entry would lead to a massacre of the refugee camps' population. In a working meeting held at 7:00 P.M. between Major General Drori and the liaison officer with the Lebanese Army at Northern Command [headquarters], the officer was told by Major General Drori that the Phalangists were about to enter the Sabra and Shatilla refugee camps; his reaction was that this was a good solution, but care should be taken that they not commit acts of murder (statement no. 4 and testimony of Major General Drori, pp. 402-403). In his statement, Captain Nahum Menahem relates that in a meeting he had with the Defense Minister on 12.9.82, he informed the Defense Minister of his opinion, which was based on considerable experience and on a study he had made of the tensions between the communities in Lebanon, that a "terrible" slaughter could ensue if Israel failed to assuage the inter-communal tensions in Lebanon (statement no. 161, p. 4). We shall mention here also articles in the press stating that excesses could be expected on the part of the Christian fighters (article in the journal *Bamahane* from 1.9.82, appended to the statement—no. 24—of the article's author, the journal's military reporter Mr. Yinon Shenkar) and that the refugee camps in Beirut were liable to undergo events exceeding what had happened at El Tel Za'atar (article in a French paper in Beirut from 20.8.82 appended to the statement, no. 76, of the journalist Mr. Strauch). We do not know whether the content of these articles was made known to the decision-makers regarding the operation of the Phalangists in West Beirut, or to those who executed the decision. We mention them solely as yet another indication that even before Bashir's assassination the possibility of the Phalangists perpetrating a massacre in the camps was not esoteric lore which need not and could not have been foreseen.

We do not say that the decision to have the Phalangists enter the camps should under no circumstances have been made and was totally unwarranted. Serious considerations existed in favor of such a decision; and on this matter we shall repeat what has already been mentioned, that an understandable desire existed to prevent I.D.F. losses in hazardous combat in a built-up area, that it was justified to demand of the Phalangists to take part in combat which they regarded as a broad opening to assume power and for the restoration of Lebanese independence, and that the Phalangists were more expert than the I.D.F. in uncovering and identifying terrorists. These are weighty considerations; and had the decision-makers and executors been aware of the danger of harm to the civilian population on the part of the Phalangists but had nevertheless, having considered all the circumstances, decided to have the Phalangists enter the camps while taking all possible steps to prevent harm coming to the civilian population, it is possible that there would be no place to be critical of them, even if ultimately it had emerged that the decision had caused undesirable results and had caused damage. However, as it transpired no examination was made of all the considerations and their ramifications; hence the appropriate orders were not issued to the executors of the decisions and insufficient heed was taken to adopt the required measures. Herein lies the basis for imputing indirect responsibility to those persons who in our view did not fulfill the obligations placed on them.

To sum up this chapter, we assert that the atrocities in the refugee camps were perpetrated by members of the Phalangists, and that absolutely no direct responsibility devolves upon Israel or upon those who acted in its behalf. At the same time, it is clear from what we have said above that the decision on the entry of the Phalangists into the refugee camps was taken without consideration of the danger—which the makers and executors of the decision were obligated to foresee as probable—that the Phalangists would commit massacres and pogroms against the inhabitants of the camps, and without an examination of the means for preventing this danger. Similarly, it is clear from the course of events that when the reports began to arrive about the actions of the Phalangists in the camps, no proper heed was taken of these reports, the correct conclusions were not drawn from them, and no energetic and immediate actions were taken to restrain the Phalangists and put a stop to their actions. This both reflects and exhausts Israel's indirect responsibility for what occurred in the refugee camps. We shall discuss the responsibility of those who acted in Israel's behalf and in its name in the following chapters.

The Responsibility of
the Political Echelon

Among those who received notices sent by the committee in accordance with Section 15(A) of the Commissions of Inquiry Law were the Prime Minister and two ministers, and in this matter no distinction was made between Cabinet ministers and officeholders and other officials. We took this course because, in our opinion, in principle, in the matter of personal responsibility, no distinction should be made between Cabinet members and others charged with personal responsibility for actions or oversights. We wish to note to the credit of the lawyers who appeared before us that none of them raised any argument to the effect that in the investigation being conducted before us, the status of Cabinet members differed from that of others. In our view, any claim that calls for a distinction of this sort is wholly untenable. We shall discuss this argument below, although it was raised not in the deliberations of the commission but outside them.

In the report of the "Commission of Inquiry—The Yom Kippur War" (henceforth the Agranat Commission), the subject of "personal responsibility of the government echelon" was discussed in Clause 30 of the partial report. It is appropriate to cite what was stated there, since we believe that it reflects the essence of the correct approach, from a legal and public standpoint, to the problem of the personal responsibility of the political echelon. The partial report of the Agranat Commission states (Section 30):

"In discussing the responsibility of ministers for an act or failure to act in which they actually or personally took part, we are obligated to stress that we consider ourselves free to draw conclusions, on the basis of our findings, that relate only to direct responsibility, and we do not see it as our task to express an opinion on what is implied by parliamentary responsibility.

"Indeed, in Israel, as in England—whence it came to us—the principle prevails that a member of the Cabinet is responsible to the elected assembly for all the administrative actions of the apparatus within his ministry, even if he was not initially aware of them and was not a party to them. However, while it is clear that this principle obligates him to report to the members of the elected assembly on such actions, including errors and failures; to reply to parliamentary questions; to defend them or to report on what has been done to correct errors—even the English experience shows that the traditions have not determined anything regarding the question of which cases of this kind require him to resign from his ministerial office; this varies, according to circumstances, from one case to the next. The main reason for this is that the question of the possible resignation of a Cabinet member in cases of this kind is essentially a political question *par excellence,* and therefore we believe that we should not deal with it. . ."

Later on in the partial report, the Agranat Commission deals (in Section 31) with the "direct personal responsibility of the Minister of Defense" and arrives at the conclusion that "according to the criterion of reasonable behavior demanded of one who holds the office of Minister of Defense, the minister was not obligated to order additional or different precautionary measures. . ."

The Agranat Commission also dealt (in Section 32 of its partial report) with the personal responsibility of the Prime Minister and arrived at the conclusion that she was not to be charged with any responsibility for her actions at the outbreak of the Yom Kippur War and afterwards.

From the above it is clear that the Agranat Commission did not in any way avoid dealing with the question of the personal responsibility of the Prime Minister and other ministers, and regarding responsibility of this kind it did not distinguish between ministers and other people whose actions were investigated by the commission. The Agranat Commission did not discuss the question of a minister's responsibility for the shortcomings and failures of the apparatus he heads and for which he should not be charged with any personal responsibility. It is not necessary to deal in this report with the question of a minister's responsibility for the failures of his apparatus which occurred without any personal blame on his part, and we shall not express an opinion on it.

The claim has been made, albeit not in the framework of the commission's deliberations, that the matter of a minister's judgment cannot serve as the subject of investigation of a commission of inquiry according to the Commissions of Inquiry Law, 1968, because a minister's judgments are political judgments; there are no set norms regarding judgments of this kind; and therefore one cannot subject such judgments to scrutiny. We reject this view. It is unfounded from both a legal and a public point of view. From a legal standpoint, it is a well known rule, and attested by many rulings of the Supreme Court (sitting in its capacity as the High Court of Justice), that any judgment of a public authority, including that of ministers, is subject to scrutiny and examination in court. Decisions made on the basis of unwarranted, irrelevant, arbitrary, unreasonable, or immaterial considerations have more than once been disqualified by the courts.

In examining the considerations that served as the basis for decisions, the court never distinguished between the obligations of a minister and those of any other public authority. The fact that there exists no hard and fast law stating that a public authority must reach its decision on the basis of correct and reasonable considerations after examining all matters brought before it in a proper manner, has not prevented the courts from imposing obligations of this sort on every public authority.

This has no bearing on the principle that the court does not substitute its own judgment for the judgment of the public authority and usually does not intervene in the policy that the authority sets for itself.

This is all the more reason for rejecting the above-mentioned view when the matter under discussion is the deliberations of a commission of inquiry that is obligated to consider not necessarily the legal aspects of the subject but also, and occasionally primarily, its public and moral aspects. The absence of any hard and fast law regarding various matters does not exempt a man whose actions are subject to the scrutiny of a commission of inquiry from accountability, from a public standpoint, for his deeds or failures that indicate inefficiency on his part, lack of proper attention to his work, or actions executed hastily, negligently, unwisely, or shortsightedly when—considering the qualifications of the man who holds a certain office and the personal qualities demanded of him in fulfilling his duties—he should have acted perspicaciously. No commission of inquiry would fulfill its role properly if it did not exercise such scrutiny, in the framework of its competence, vis-à-vis any man whose actions and failures were under scrutiny, regardless of his position and public standing.

In conclusion, regarding personal responsibility, we will not draw a distinction between the political echelon and any other echelon.

Personal Responsibility
In accordance with a resolution adopted by the Commission on 24.11.82, notices were sent under Section 15(A) of the Commissions of Inquiry Law, 1968, to nine persons regarding the harm liable to be done to them by the inquiry and its results. We shall now consider the matter of each of those who received such a notice.

The Prime Minister, Mr. Menachem Begin
The notice sent to the Prime Minister, Mr. Menachem Begin, stated that he was liable to be harmed if the commission were to determine "that the Prime Minister did not properly weigh the part to be played by Lebanese forces during and in the wake of the I.D.F.'s entry into West Beirut, and disregarded the danger of acts of revenge and bloodshed by these forces vis-à-vis the population in the refugee camps."

The Prime Minister's response to the notice stated that in the conversations between him and the Defense Minister in which the decision was taken to have I.D.F. units enter West Beirut, and in the conversations he had held with the Chief of Staff during the night between 14.9.82 and 15.9.82, nothing at all was said about a possible operation by the Lebanese Forces.

The Prime Minister testified that only in the Cabinet session of 16.9.82 did he hear about the agreement with the Phalangists that they would operate in the camps, and that until then, in all the conversations he had held with the Defense Minister and with the Chief of Staff, nothing had been said about the role of the Phalangists or their participation in the operations in West Beirut. He added that since this matter had not come up in the reports he received from the Defense Minister and the Chief of Staff, he had raised no questions about it. The Prime Minister's remarks in this regard are consistent with the testimony of the Defense Minister and the Chief of Staff, and with the existing documents concerning the content of the conversations with the Prime Minister. We have described above the two conversations between the Prime Minister and the Defense Minister from the roof of the forward command post on Wednesday, 15.9.82, in the morning hours. According to the testimony and the notes of those conversations, the matter of the Phalangists was not mentioned in them at all. In a further conversation between the Defense Minister and the Prime Minister, on Wednesday at 18:00 hours, nothing was said about the participation of the Phalangists in the entry into Beirut. Similarly, on Thursday, 16.9.82, when the Defense Minister spoke by phone with the Prime Minister during the discussion in the Defense Minister's office, the Defense Minister said nothing about the Phalangists. According to the content of the conversation (see Exhibit 27), his report to the Prime Minister was in an optimistic vein: that the fighting had ended, the I.D.F. held all the key points, and it was all over. The only mention of the camps in that conversation was that they were encircled.

We may certainly wonder that the participation of the Phalangists in the entry to West Beirut and their being given the task of "mopping up" the camps seemed so unimportant that the Defense Minister did not inform the Prime Minister of it and did not get his assent for the decision; however, that question does not bear on the responsibility of the Prime Minister. What is clear is that the Prime Minister was not a party to the decision to have the Phalangists move into the camps, and that he received no report about that decision until the Cabinet session on the evening of 16.9.82.

We do not believe that we ought to be critical of the Prime Minister because he did not on his own initiative take an interest in the details of the operation of the entry into West Beirut, and did not discover, through his own questions, that the Phalangists were taking part in that operation. The tasks of the Prime Minister are many and diverse, and he was entitled to rely on the optimistic and calming report of the Defense Minister that the entire operation was proceeding without any hitches and in the most satisfactory manner.

We have cited above passages from remarks made at the Cabinet session of 16.9.82, during which the Prime Minister learned that the Phalangists had that evening begun to operate in the camps. Neither in that meeting nor afterward did the Prime Minister raise any opposition or objection to the entry of the Phalangists into the camps. Nor did he react to the remarks of Deputy Prime Minister Levy which contained a warning of the danger to be expected from the Phalangists' entry into the camps. According to the Prime Minister's testimony, "No one conceived that atrocities would be committed . . . simply, none of us, no minister, none of the other participants supposed such a thing. . ." (p. 767). The Prime Minister attached no importance to Minister Levy's remarks because the latter did not ask for a discussion or a vote on this subject. When Minister Levy made his remarks, the Prime Minister was busy formulating the concluding resolution of the meeting, and for this reason as well, he did not pay heed to Minister Levy's remarks.

We have already said above, when we discussed the question of indirect responsibility, that in our view, because of things that were well known to all, it should have been foreseen that the danger of a massacre existed if the Phalangists were to enter the camps without measures being taken to prevent them from committing acts such as these. We are unable to accept the Prime Minister's remarks that he was absolutely unaware of such a danger. According to what he himself said, he told the Chief of Staff on the night between 14 and 15 September 1982, in explaining the decision to have the I.D.F. occupy positions in West Beirut, that this was being done "in order to protect the Moslems from the vengeance of the Phalangists," and he could well suppose that after the assassination of Bashir, the Phalangists' beloved leader, they would take revenge on the terrorists. The Prime Minister was aware of the mutual massacres committed in Lebanon during the civil war, and of the Phalangists' feelings of hate for the Palestinians, whom the Phalangists held responsible for all the calamities that befell their land. The purpose of the I.D.F.'s entry into West Beirut—in order to prevent bloodshed—was also stressed by the Prime Minister in his meeting with Ambassador Draper on 15.9.82. We are prepared to believe the Prime Minister that, being preoccupied at the Cabinet session with formulating the resolution, he did not pay heed to the remarks of Minister Levy, which were uttered following lengthy reviews and discussions. However, in view of what has already been noted above regarding foresight and probability of acts of slaughter, we are unable to accept the position of the Prime Minister that no one imagined that what happened was liable to happen, or what follows from his remarks: that this possibility did not have to be foreseen when the decision was taken to have the Phalangists move into the camps.

As noted, the Prime Minister first heard about the Phalangists' entry into the camps about 36 hours after the decision to that effect was taken, and did not learn of the decision until the Cabinet session. When he heard about the Phalangists' entry into the camps, it had already taken place. According to the "rosy" reports the Prime Minister received from the Defense Minister and the Chief of Staff, the Prime Minister was entitled to assume at that time that all the operations in West Beirut had been performed in the best possible manner and had nearly been concluded. We believe that in these circumstances it was not incumbent upon the Prime Minister to object to the Phalangists' entry into the camps or to order their removal. On the other hand, we find no reason to exempt the Prime Minister from responsibility for not having evinced, during or after the Cabinet session, any interest in the Phalangists' actions in the camps. It has already been noted above that no report about the Phalangists' operations reached the Prime Minister, except perhaps for the complaint regarding the Gaza Hospital, until he heard the BBC broadcast towards evening on Saturday. For two days after the Prime Minister heard about the Phalangists' entry, he showed absolutely no interest in their actions in the camps. This indifference would have been justifiable if we were to accept the Prime Minister's position that it was impossible and unnecessary to foresee the possibility that the Phalangists would commit acts of revenge; but we have already explained above that according to what the Prime Minister knew, according to what he heard in the Thursday Cabinet session, and according to what he said about the purpose of the move into Beirut, such a possibility was not unknown to him. It may be assumed that a manifestation of interest by him in this matter, after he had learned of the Phalangists' entry, would have increased the alertness of the Defense Minister and the Chief of Staff to the need to take appropriate measures to meet the expected danger. The Prime Minister's lack of involvement in the entire matter casts on him a certain degree of responsibility.

The Minister of Defense, Mr. Ariel Sharon
The notice sent to the Minister of Defense under Section 15(A) stated that the Minister of Defense might be harmed if the commission determined that he ignored or disregarded the danger of acts of revenge or bloodshed perpetrated by Lebanese forces against the population of the refugee camps in Beirut and did not order the adoption of the withdrawal of the Lebanese forces from the refugee camps as quickly as possible and the adoption of measures to protect the population in the camps when information reached him about the acts of killing or excesses that were perpetrated by the Lebanese forces.

In his testimony before us, and in statements he issued beforehand, the Minister of Defense also adopted the position that no one had imagined the Phalangists would carry out a massacre in the camps and that it was a tragedy that could not be foreseen. It was stressed by the Minister of Defense in his testimony, and argued in his behalf, that the director of Military Intelligence, who spent time with him and maintained contact with him on the days prior to the Phalangists' entry into the camps and at the time of their entry into the camps, did not indicate the danger of a massacre, and that no warning was received from the Mossad, which was responsible for the liaison with the Phalangists and also had special knowledge of the character of this force.

It is true that no clear warning was provided by Military Intelligence or the Mossad about what might happen if the Phalangist forces entered the camps, and we will relate to this matter when we discuss the responsibility of the director of Military Intelligence and the head of the Mossad. But in our view, even without such warning, it is impossible to justify the Minister of Defense's disregard of the danger of a massacre. We will not repeat here what we have already said about the widespread knowledge regarding the Phalangists' combat ethics, their feelings of hatred toward the Palestinians, and their leaders' plans for the future of the Palestinians when said leaders would assume power. Besides this general knowledge, the Defense Minister also had special reports from his not inconsiderable [number of] meetings with the Phalangist heads before Bashir's assassination.

Giving the Phalangists the possibility of entering the refugee camps without taking measures for continuous and concrete supervision of their actions there could have created a grave danger for the civilian population in the camps even if they had been given such a possibility before Bashir's assassination; thus this danger was certainly to have been anticipated—and it was imperative to have foreseen it—after Bashir's assassination. The fact that it was not clear which organization had caused Bashir's death was of no importance at all, given the known frame of mind among the combatant camps in Lebanon. In the circumstances that prevailed after Bashir's assassination, no prophetic powers were required to know that concrete danger of acts of slaughter existed when the Phalangists were moved into the camps without the I.D.F.'s being with them in that operation and without the I.D.F. being able to maintain effective and ongoing supervision of their actions there. The sense of danger should have been in the consciousness of every knowledgeable person who was close to this subject, and certainly in the consciousness of the Defense Minister, who took an active part in everything relating to the war. His involvement in the war was deep, and the connection with the Phalangists was under his constant care. If in fact the Defense Minister, when he decided that the Phalangists would enter the camps without the I.D.F. taking part in the operation, did not think that that decision could bring about the very disaster that in fact occurred, the only possible explanation for this is that he disregarded any apprehensions about what was to be expected because the advantages—which we have already noted—to be gained from the Phalangists' entry into the camps distracted him from the proper consideration in this instance.

As a politician responsible for Israel's security affairs, and as a minister who took an active part in directing the political and military moves in the war in Lebanon, it was the duty of the Defense Minister to take into account all the reasonable considerations for and against having the Phalangists enter the camps, and not to disregard entirely the serious consideration mitigating against such an action, namely that the Phalangists were liable to commit atrocities and that it was necessary to forestall this possibility as a humanitarian obligation and also to prevent the political damage it would entail. From the Defense Minister himself we know that this consideration did not concern him in the least, and that this matter, with all its ramifications, was neither discussed nor examined in the meetings and discussions held by the Defense Minister. In our view, the Minister of Defense made a grave mistake when he ignored the danger of acts of revenge and bloodshed by the Phalangists against the population in the refugee camps.

We have already said above that we do not assert that the decision to have the Phalangists enter the camps should under no circumstances ever have been made. It appears to us that no complaints could be addressed to the Defense Minister in this matter if such a decision had been taken after all the relevant considerations had been examined; however, if the decision were taken with the awareness that the risk of harm to the inhabitants existed, the obligation existed to adopt measures which would ensure effective and ongoing supervision by the I.D.F. over the actions of the Phalangists at the site, in such a manner as to prevent the danger or at least reduce it considerably. The Defense Minister issued no order regarding the adoption of such measures. We shall not dwell here on what steps might have been taken; this we shall consider below. Regarding the responsibility of the Minister of Defense, it is sufficient to assert that he issued no order to the I.D.F. to adopt suitable measures. Similarly, in his meeting with the Phalangist commanders, the Defense Minister made no attempt to point out to them the gravity of the danger that their men would commit acts of slaughter. Although it is not certain that remarks to this effect by the Defense Minister would have prevented the acts of massacre, they might have had an effect on the Phalangist commanders who, out of concern for their political interests, would have imposed appropriate supervision over their people and seen to it that they did not exceed regular combat operations. It was related above that a few hours after the Phalangists entered the camps, soldiers at the site asked what to do with the people who had fallen into their hands, and the replies they were given not only did not bar them from harming those people, but even urged them to do so. It is a highly reasonable assumption that had the commanders who gave that reply heard from the Defense Minister or from higher Phalangist commanders a clear and explicit order barring harm to civilians and spelling out the damage this was liable to cause the Phalangists, their reply to these questions would have been different.

Had it become clear to the Defense Minister that no real supervision could be exercised over the Phalangist force that entered the camps with the I.D.F.'s assent, his duty would have been to prevent their entry. The usefulness of the Phalangists' entry into the camps was wholly disproportionate to the damage their entry could cause if it were uncontrolled. A good many people who heard about the Phalangists' entry into the camps were aware of this even before the first reports arrived about the massacre. The Chief of Staff in effect also held the same opinion, as emerges from his reply to a question whether he would have issued orders for additional measures to be taken or would have sufficed with the steps that were in fact taken, had it been expected that the Phalangists would commit excesses. He replied as follows (p. 1677):

"No, if I had expected that this was liable to happen, or if someone had warned me that this was liable to happen, they would not have entered the camps."

In reply to another question, whether he would have taken additional measures, the Chief of Staff said:

"They would not have entered the camps; I would not have allowed them to enter the camps."

Asked if he would not have allowed the Phalangists to enter the camps despite the aim of having them operate together with the I.D.F. and spare the I.D.F. losses, the Chief of Staff replied:

"Then maybe we should have acted differently, by closing the camps, by surrounding them, or bringing them to surrender in another week or in another few days, or shelling them with all our might from the air and with artillery. As for me, if I had anticipated that this is what would happen, or if such a warning had been given, they would not have entered the camps."

And the Chief of Staff added that if he had suspected or feared that what happened would happen, "They would not have entered the camps at all, they would not have come anywhere near the camps." We quote these remarks here in order to show that despite the usefulness of having the Phalangists enter the camps, that step should have been abandoned if a massacre could not have been prevented using the means in the I.D.F.'s hands.

We do not accept the contention that the Defense Minister did not need to fear that the Phalangists would commit acts of killing because in all outward aspects they looked like a disciplined and organized army. It could not be inferred from the Phalangists' orderly military organization that their attitude toward human life and to the non-combatant population had basically changed. It might perhaps be inferred from their military organization that the soldiers would heed the orders of their commanders and not break discipline; but at the very least, care should have been taken that the commanders were imbued with the awareness that no excesses were to be committed and that they give their men unequivocal orders to this effect. The routine warnings that I.D.F. commanders issued to the Phalangists, which were of the same kind as were routinely issued to I.D.F. troops, could not have had any concrete effect.

We shall remark here that it is ostensibly puzzling that the Defense Minister did not in any way make the Prime Minister privy to the decision on having the Phalangists enter the camps.

It is our view that responsibility is to be imputed to the Minister of Defense for having disregarded the danger of acts of vengeance and bloodshed by the Phalangists against the population of the refugee camps, and having failed to take this danger into account when he decided to have the Phalangists enter the camps. In addition, responsibility is to be imputed to the Minister of Defense for not ordering appropriate measures for preventing or reducing the danger of massacre as a condition for the Phalangists' entry into the camps. These blunders constitute the non-fulfillment of a duty with which the Defense Minister was charged.

We do not believe that responsibility is to be imputed to the Defense Minister for not ordering the removal of the Phalangists from the camps when the first reports reached him about the acts of killing being committed there. As was detailed above, such reports initially reached the Defense Minister on Friday evening; but at the same time, he had heard from the Chief of Staff that the Phalangists' operation had been halted, that they had been ordered to leave the camps, and that their departure would be effected by 5:00 A.M. Saturday. These preventive steps might well have seemed sufficient to the Defense Minister at that time, and it was not his duty to order additional steps to be taken, or to have the departure time moved up, a step which was of doubtful feasibility.

The Foreign Minister, Mr. Yitzhak Shamir

The Foreign Minister, Mr. Yitzhak Shamir, was sent a notice under Section 15(A) that he might be harmed if the commission determined that after he heard from Minister Zipori on 17.9.82 of the report regarding the Phalangists' actions in the refugee camps, he did not take the appropriate steps to clarify whether this information was based in fact and did not bring the information to the knowledge of the Prime Minister or the Minister of Defense.

In the memorandum that the Foreign Minister submitted to us in response to the aforementioned notice, he explained that what he had heard from Minister Zipori about the "unruliness" of the Phalangists did not lead him to understand that it was a matter of a massacre; he thought, rather, that it was a matter of fighting against terrorists. Since he knew that many of them had remained in Beirut, together with their weapons, he could have had the impression from Minister Zipori's statement that perhaps the Phalangists' combat operations were carried out in a manner that differed from the way a battle was conducted by the I.D.F, but he did not understand that a massacre of civilians, women and children, was taking place. The Foreign Minister also explained his attitude to Minister Zipori's statement by stating that he knew that Minister Zipori had been long and consistently opposed to cooperation with the Phalangists, and he was also known in the Cabinet as a constant critic of the Minister of Defense, the Chief of Staff, and their actions. For these reasons the Foreign Minister restricted himself to asking a member of his ministry's staff whether there was any news from West Beirut and satisfied himself that there was no need for further investigation after the Minister of Defense and others responsible for security affairs came to his office and did not mention that anything extraordinary had occurred in Beirut.

It is not easy to decide between the conflicting versions of what Minister Zipori said to the Foreign Minister. We tend to the opinion that in the telephone conversation Minister Zipori spoke of a "slaughter" being perpetrated by the Phalangists, and it is possible that he also spoke of "unruliness." He had heard from the journalist Ze'ev Schiff of reports that a massacre was going on in the camps and had treated Schiff's information seriously; and it is difficult to find a reason why he would not have told the Foreign Minister what he had heard when the point of the telephone communication was to inform the Foreign Minister what he had learned from Schiff. Mr. Schiff, in a statement he has submitted, confirms Minister Zipori's version. Nevertheless, we are unable to rule out the possibility that the Foreign Minister did not catch or did not properly understand the significance of what he heard from Minister Zipori. The Foreign Minister likewise did not conceal that in relating to what Minister Zipori had told him, he was influenced by his knowledge that Minister Zipori was opposed to the policy of the Minister of Defense and the Chief of Staff regarding the war in Lebanon, and particularly to cooperation with the Phalangists.

The phenomenon that came to light in this case—namely, that the statement of one minister to another did not receive the attention it deserved because of faulty relations between members of the Cabinet— is regrettable and worrisome. The impression we got is that the Foreign Minister did not make any real attempt to check whether there was anything in what he had heard from Minister Zipori on the Phalangists' operations in the camps because he had an *a priori* skeptical attitude toward the statements of the minister who reported this information to him. It is difficult to find a justification for such disdain for information that came from a member of the Cabinet, especially under the circumstances in which the information was reported. As stated, the conversation between the two ministers was preceded by a Cabinet meeting on 16.9.82 at which Minister Levy had expressed a warning of the danger involved in sending the Phalangists into the camps. That Friday was the end of a week in which dramatic events had occurred, and the situation as a whole was permeated with tension and dangers. In this state of affairs, it might have been expected that the Foreign Minister, by virtue of his position, would display sensitivity and alertness to what he had heard from another minister—even if we were to accept unconditionally his statement that the point under discussion was only the "unruliness" of the Phalangists. The Foreign Minister should at least have called the Defense Minister's attention to the information he had received and not contented himself with asking someone in his office whether any new information had come in from Beirut and with the expectation that those people coming to his office would know what was going on and would tell him if anything out of the ordinary had happened. In our view, the Foreign Minister erred in not taking any measures after the conversation with Minister Zipori in regard to what he had heard from Zipori about the Phalangist actions in the camps.

The Chief of Staff, Lieutenant General Rafael Eitan

The notice sent to the Chief of Staff, Lieutenant General Rafael Eitan, according to Section 15(A), detailed a number of findings or conclusions that might be harmful to the Chief of Staff if the commission established them.

The first point in the notice has to do with the Chief of Staff disregarding the danger of acts of vengeance and bloodshed being perpetrated by the Phalangists against the population of the refugee camps and his failure to take the appropriate measures to prevent this danger. In this matter, the Chief of Staff took a position similar to that of the Minister of Defense which was discussed above and which we have rejected. The Chief of Staff stated in his testimony before us that it had never occurred to him that the Phalangists would perpetrate acts of revenge and bloodshed in the camps. He justified this lack of foresight be citing the experience of the past, whereby massacres were perpetrated by the Christians only before the "Peace for Galilee" War and only in response

75

to the perpetration of a massacre by the Muslims against the Christian population, and by citing the disciplined conduct of the Phalangists while carrying out certain operations after the I.D.F.'s entry into Lebanon. The Chief of Staff also noted the development of the Phalangists from a militia into an organized and orderly military force, as well as the interest of the Phalangist leadership, and first and foremost of Bashir Jemayel, in behaving moderately toward the Muslim population so that the president-elect could be accepted by all the communities in Lebanon. Finally, the Chief of Staff also noted, in justifying his position, that none of the experts in the I.D.F. or in the Mossad had expressed any reservations about the planned operation in the camps.

We are not prepared to accept these explanations. In our view, none of these reasons had the power to cancel out the serious concern that in going into the refugee camps, the Phalangist forces would perpetrate indiscriminate acts of killing. We rejected arguments of this kind in the part of this report that deals with indirect responsibility, as well as in our discussion of the responsibility borne by the Minister of Defense, and the reasons we presented there likewise hold for the Chief of Staff's position. Here we will restrict ourselves to brief reasoning.

Past experience in no way justified the conclusion that the entry of the Phalangists into the camps posed no danger. The Chief of Staff was well aware that the Phalangists were full of feelings of hatred toward the Palestinians and that their feelings had not changed since the "Peace for Galilee" War. The isolated actions in which the Phalangists had participated during the war took place under conditions that were completely different from those which arose after the murder of Bashir Jemayel; and as one could see from the nature of [those] operations, in the past there had been no case in which an area populated by Palestinian refugees had been turned over to the exclusive control of the Phalangists. On a number of occasions, the Chief of Staff had harsh and clear-cut things to say about the manner of fighting between the factions and communities in Lebanon, and about the concept of vengeance rooted in them; and in this matter we need only refer to the detailed facts presented in this report. We have already said a number of times that the traumatic event of the murder of Bashir Jemayel and of a group of Phalangists was sufficient reason to whip up the Phalangists. It is difficult to understand how it was possible to justify ignoring the effect of this event on arousing a feeling of vengeance and hatred toward all those who were inimical to the Phalangists, and first and foremost the Palestinians. The consideration that the military organization of the Phalangists and their orderly and disciplined appearance attested to a change in their mode of fighting was specious, and we have already pointed this out.

The absence of a warning from experts cannot serve as an explanation for ignoring the danger of a massacre. The Chief of Staff should have known and foreseen—by virtue of common knowledge, as well as the special information at his disposal—that there was a possibility of harm to the population in the camps at the hands of the Phalangists. Even if the experts did not fulfill their obligation, this does not absolve the Chief of Staff of responsibility.

The decision to send the Phalangistss into the camps was taken by the Minister of Defense and the Chief of Staff, and the Chief of Staff must be viewed as a partner to this decision and as bearing responsibility both for its adoption and for its implementation. The Chief of Staff did not express any opposition to or reservation about the decision to the Minister of Defense, and no one disputed that it was taken with his consent. There is no reason to doubt that had the Chief of Staff expressed opposition or reservation, this fact would have borne serious weight in the consideration of the decision; and had there been a difference of opinion between him and the Minister of Defense, he could easily have brought the matter before the Prime Minister for his decision. It emerges quite clearly from the Chief of Staff's testimony, as cited above, that his opposition to sending the Phalangists into the camps would have meant that they would not have been sent in, and other means (which he detailed in the statement cited above) would have been adopted for taking control of the camps.

If the Chief of Staff did not imagine at all that the entry of the Phalangists into the camps posed a danger to the civilian population, his thinking on this matter constitutes a disregard of important considerations that he should have taken into account. Moreover, considering the Chief of Staff's own statements quoted above, it is difficult to avoid the conclusion that the Chief of Staff ignored this danger out of an awareness that there were great advantages to sending the Phalangists into the camps, and perhaps also out of a hope that in the final analysis, the Phalangist excesses would not be on a large scale. This conclusion is likewise prompted by the Chief of Staff's behavior during later stages, once reports began to come in about the Phalangists' excesses in the camps.

It has been argued by the Chief of Staff, and in his behalf, that appropriate steps were taken to avoid the danger. A similar claim has been made by Major General Drori and Brigadier General Yaron. In our opinion, this claim is unfounded.

As stated, one of the precautions was a lookout posted on the roof of the forward command post and on another roof nearby. It may be that this lookout was of value in obtaining certain military information on combat operations, but it was worthless in terms of obtaining information on the Phalangists' operations within the camps. Another step was taken to obtain information on exchanges over the communications sets between the Phalangist forces in the field and their commanders. It is difficult to regard this step as an efficient way to discover what was going on in the camps, because it was based on the assumption that what was said over the communications network would provide an accurate picture not only of the combat operations but also of any atrocities, and this assumption was not sufficiently grounded. It is true that the first reports of the massacres came from this source of information, but that was merely fortuitous; and just as questions had been asked about the fate of 45 to 50 people, it could have happened that such questions would not have gone over the communications network. As stated, the fact of 300 dead was not discovered as a result of listening in on the communications set; and it is a fact that whatever was said over these sets did not reveal the fact that the massacre of hundreds of people was going on in the camps. The final means whereby it was hoped that the Phalangists' operations in the camps would be revealed was by placing a Phalangist liaison officer on the roof of the forward comand post and a liaison officer from the Mossad in the Phalangist headquarters. The obtaining of information from these two sources was likewise based on unfounded assumptions. As for the Phalangist officer, there was no reason to believe that on his own initiative, he would tell the I.D.F. officers about the Phalangist operations, for he knew that the I.D.F. would vigorously oppose them if word of such operations came to its attention. While Phalangist liaison officer G. did tell of 300 dead, this was evidently a slip of the tongue on his part, for he immediately tried to play down the assessment by decreasing the number of casualties to 120. No information was received from the Mossad liaison officer; and the hope that he would be able to supply information of this sort was based on the unrealistic expectation that the Phalangist commanders would let him in on all the information that came in about the Phalangists' actions, even if it was a report on an action they knew the I.D.F. would vigorously oppose.

We asked the witnesses why an I.D.F. liaison officer was not attached to the Phalangist force that entered the camps, and we received the reply that there were two reasons: first, the point was that the I.D.F. should not enter the refugee camps, and the presence of an I.D.F. liaison officer would contradict that point; second there was fear for the life of any such liaison officer, for obvious reasons. We are prepared to accept this explanation and have no criticism of the fact that this step was not adopted. On the other hand, no explanation was given for failing to provide special briefings to the I.D.F. units that were in the vicinity of the camps—something which should have been done, considering the importance of the matter.

The claim that every possible step was taken to obtain detailed information on the excesses of the Phalangists—in the event that such excesses would take place—is not congruent with the claim that such excesses were not foreseen at all. But we do not wish to go into this logical contradiction, as in any case it is clear that the steps which were adopted fell far short of satisfying the need to know what was going on in the camps; and in fact, the truth about what was happening there only came out after the Phalangists left the camps.

We find that the Chief of Staff did not consider the danger of acts of vengeance and bloodshed being perpetrated against the population of the refugee camps in Beirut; he did not order the adoption of the appropriate steps to avoid this danger; and his failure to do so is tantamount to a breach of duty that was incumbent upon the Chief of Staff.

The other matter for which a notice was sent to the Chief of Staff under Section 15(A) was that when reports reached him about acts of killing or actions that deviated from usual combat operations, he did not check the veracity of these reports and the scope of these actions and did not order the cessation of the operations, the removal of the Phalangists from the camps as quickly as possible, and the adoption of steps to protect the population of the camps. In a meeting with the Phalangist commanders on the morning of 17.9.82, he approved the continuation of their operations until the morning of 18.9.82 and ordered that they be provided with assistance for that purpose.

As related in the description of the events in this report, the Chief of Staff first heard of the excesses perpetrated by the Phalangists when Major General Drori contacted him by phone on Friday morning. The Chief of Staff did not ask Major General Drori at that time what he knew about the excesses and what moved him to halt the Phalangist operation; and one should not take him to task for this, because he had decided to go to Beirut and preferred to clarify the matter during a personal visit, rather than try to clear it up in a phone conversation. On the other hand, it is difficult to understand or justify the Chief of Staff's actions after he reached Beirut, and especially during the meeting with the Phalangist commanders. Upon reaching Beirut, the Chief of Staff heard from Major General Drori what the latter knew about the Phalangist actions; he contented himself with this report and asked no question about this matter either of Major General Drori or of Brigadier General Yaron. If it is still possible to comprehend this reticence as stemming from the Chief of Staff's expectation that he would hear more exact details during his meeting with the Phalangist commanders, what took place at that meeting raises questions to which we have not found a reasonable answer. The Chief of Staff did not raise with the Phalangist commanders any question about the aberrant operations or the grave actions that might have been perpetrated in the camps. It is clear from his testimony that he thought that if any such actions had been perpetrated, the Phalangist commanders would have told him about them on their own initiative. There was no real basis for this naive belief. It is impossible to understand how the Chief of Staff concluded, from the fact that the Phalangist commanders told him nothing about the operations against the civilian population in the camps, that the suspicions that had arisen about those actions had no basis in reality.

The outstanding impression that emerges from the Chief of Staff's testimony is that his refraining from raising the issue of the Phalangists' excesses against the population in the camps stemmed from a fear of offending their honor; but this fear was out of place and should not have been a cause for the lack of any clarification of what had happened, when the Chief of Staff had gotten reports that should have served as a warning about the grave harm caused to the population in the camps and when, as a result of these reports, Major General Drori had issued an order to halt the advance of the Phalangists. Not only did the Chief of Staff not raise the subject of the Phalangists' behavior in the camps at the meeting which was called to clarify what was happening in the camps, but he expressed his satisfaction with the Phalangist operation and agreed to their request to provide them with tractors so they could complete their operations by Saturday morning. It is difficult to avoid the conclusion that this conduct on the Chief of Staff's part during the meeting at the Phalangists' headquarters stemmed from his disregard of the suspicions that the Phalangists were perpetrating acts of slaughter, and this disregard went so deep that even the information that had arrived in the meanwhile and reached the Chief of Staff did not shake it.

It emerges from the Chief of Staff's testimony that after the meeting with the Phalangists, he felt assured that everything was proceeding properly, that nothing out of the ordinary had happened that would require the immediate removal of the Phalangists from the camps, and that there was nothing wrong with—and perhaps there was benefit to be derived from—their completing their operation through Saturday morning. It is impossible to reconcile what we heard from the Chief of Staff regarding this matter with what he told the Minister of Defense in a phone conversation when he returned to Israel. We have already established above that in this conversation, the Chief of Staff told the Minister of Defense things about the conduct of the Phalangists that could have led the Minister of Defense to understand that the Phalangists had perpetrated the murder of civilians in the camps. But even if we go by the Chief of Staff's version of that conversation, according to which he said only that the Phalangists had "overdone it," it is difficult to reconcile this statement with the absence of all suspicion on his part regarding what had happened in the camps and the possibility of further similar actions.

Likewise, after the meeting, the Chief of Staff did not issue an order to Major General Drori or Brigadier General Yaron to prevent the entry of additional Phalangist forces or to send in or replace [Phalangist] forces, because he did not have the impression that there was any reason to stop them.

In our opinion, after the Chief of Staff received the information from Major General Drori in a telephone conversation that the Phalangists had "overdone it" and Major General Drori had halted their operation, this information should have alerted him to the danger that acts of slaughter were being perpetrated in the camps and made him aware of his obligation to take appropriate steps to clarify the matter and prevent the continuation of such actions if the information proved to be of substance. Toward that end, the Chief of Staff should have held a detailed clarification [session] with Major General Drori, Brigadier General Yaron, and other officers of the division, as well as with the Phalangist commanders, immediately upon his arrival in Beirut. If, as a result of this clarification, he was not satisfied that excesses had not been committed in the camps, he should have ordered the immediate removal of the Phalangist forces from the camp, admonished the Phalangist commanders about the aberrant actions, and demanded that they issue immediate orders to their forces to refrain from any act that would cause harm to civilians while they were still in the camp. None of these things was done by the Chief of Staff. On the contrary, the Phalangist commanders could have gotten the impression from the Chief of Staff's words and from his agreement to supply them with tractors that they could continue their operations in the camp without interference until Saturday morning and that no reports of excesses had reached the I.D.F.—and if they had reached the I.D.F., they had not roused any sharp reaction.

We determine that the Chief of Staff's inaction, described above, and his order to provide the Phalangist forces with tractors, or a tractor, constitute a breach of duty and dereliction of the duty incumbent upon the Chief of Staff.

Director of Military Intelligence,
Major General Yehoshua Saguy

In the notice sent to the director of Military Intelligence, Major General Yehoshua Saguy, nonfulfillment of duty was ascribed to him because he did not give sufficient attention to the decision regarding sending the Phalangists into the camps and did not warn after the murder of Bashir Jemayel of the danger of acts of revenge and bloodshed by these forces against the Palestinian population in West Beirut, and especially in the refugee camps.

The director of Military Intelligence testified that he did not know at all about the decision regarding the sending of the Phalangists into the camps and did not hear about the role assigned to the Phalangists in connection with the entry into Beirut until he discovered the matter in the cable regarding the 300 killed on Friday morning (17.9.82). We find it difficult to accept this claim. The decision regarding the sending of the Phalangists into the camps was discussed on the roof of the forward command post on Wednesday morning, 15.9.82, in conversations between the Minister of Defense, the Chief of Staff and Major General Drori; and we find it hard to believe that a decision discussed in these conversations did not at all reach the director of Military Intelligence, who was present on the roof of the forward command post. According to the description of the detailed discussions which were held that morning on the roof of the forward command post, the director of Military Intelligence had ample opportunities to hear on that occasion about the plans regarding the participation of the Phalangists in the entry to Beirut and about the role assigned to them. If indeed the director of Military Intelligence did not hear then about the plan to send the Phalangists into the camps, then the only reason that can be given for this is that he was completely indifferent to what was being said and what was happening at that time on the roof of the forward command post, and showed no interest in the subjects which by virtue of his position should have interested him.

From the forward command post the director of Military Intelligence traveled together with the Defense Minister to the meeting at Phalangist headquarters; and there the Defense Minister said that the Phalangist forces would enter West Beirut—though he apparently did not say explicitly that they would enter the camps. Regarding this meeting, Major General Saguy testified that it seems to him that it was said that the Phalangists should participate in something, but he does not remember exactly (p. 1561). After that meeting as well, the director of Military Intelligence evinced no special interest in the question of what would be the role of the Phalangists in the entry into Beirut. He spent a considerable amount of time with the Defense Minister and did not find it necessary to pose any question to him regarding this matter. An additional meeting in which the director of Military Intelligence could have, if he had wanted to, obtained information on the plans regarding the roles of the Phalangists in West Beirut took place at a gas station, after the condolence call in Bikfaya, when Major General Drori reported to the Defense Minister on the course of events during the I.D.F.'s entry into Beirut and showed him maps. This opportunity was also missed, for some reason by the director of Military Intelligence. An additional discussion in which the director of Military Intelligence participated and in which the entry of the Phalangists into the camps was explicitly mentioned was in the meeting at the Defense Minister's office on Thursday, 16.9.82, at 10:00 A.M. According to Major General Saguy he did not pay attention to things said at that meeting on the sending of the Phalangists into the camps. The inattention [displayed] in this meeting as well is surprising and inexplicable. Major General Saguy was present at the beginning of the Cabinet meeting on Thursday evening and left the meeting a short time after it had begun. It has not been explained why Major General Saguy did not demonstrate sufficient interest in the role of the Phalangists in the entry into West Beirut and left the place without even trying to ascertain from anyone present there who knew what was happening in Beirut what the plan was for involving the Phalangists. To all this it should be added that already on Wednesday, 15.9.82, the assistant for research to the director of Military Intelligence heard at a meeting in the office of the Deputy Chief of Staff about the plan that the Phalangists would enter the camps (p. 7 in Exhibit 130).

We cannot believe that no information about the plan to send the Phalangists into the camps reached the director of Military Intelligence until Friday morning, keeping in mind that he was present at a number of meetings in which this plan was mentioned and he had ample opportunity to ascertain the role given to the Phalangists. Even if we were to unreservedly accept Major Saguy's testimony in this matter, his statements would have been surprising. The director of Military Intelligence, who is required to provide an intelligence assessment regarding the Phalangists, knows that the I.D.F. is entering Beirut, knows that in the past there had been complaints about the non-involvement of the Phalangists in the fighting, hears, at the latest on Wednesday morning during the meeting at Phalangist headquarters, that these forces will cooperate with the I.D.F. in the entry into West Beirut, he does not demonstrate any interest and does not raise any questions as to the role assigned them and does not make any comment to the Defense Minister or the Chief of Staff on this matter in the meetings in which he participated. The picture received according to the testimony of Major General Saguy himself is of indifference and conspicuous lack of concern, of shutting of eyes and ears to a matter regarding which it was incumbent on the director of the intelligence arm of the I.D.F. to open his eyes and listen well to all that was discussed and decided.

The only explanation which can be found for the aforementioned behavior of the director of Military Intelligence apparently lies in the fact that the approach of the director of Military Intelligence to the Phalangists and to cooperation between Israel and these forces was much more skeptical than the sympathetic approach of the Mossad, and that he knew that the Defense Minister, Chief of Staff and perhaps also the Prime Minister rejected Military Intelligence's approach in favor of the Mossad's approach. Therefore, the director of Military Intelligence was satisfied with Intelligence reports compiled and sent on his behalf, in which, according to his claim, there is sufficient warning of the dangers to be expected from cooperation with the Phalangists.

In our opinion, the director of Military Intelligence did not fulfill his testified, was given rather weakly. According to Major General Saguy's testimony (pp. 105-106), he said in a telephone conversation with the Defense Minister on the night of 14.9.82, when it became clear that Bashir had been killed, that there were two possibilities: one, that there would be acts of revenge on the part of the Phalangists: and two, that they [the Phalangists] would fall apart. It is difficult to view these vague statements as a substantial warning. On 15.9.82, at about 18:00 hours, Intelligence Branch prepared a document (Exhibit 26) bearing the title, "Main Emphases for Situation Assessment," and the only thing said there regarding the danger of acts of revenge by the Phalangists is that the I.D.F.'s entry into West Beirut could "be received by some of the parties involved, and perhaps even among some of the Muslim elements, as a development which might contribute, at least temporarily, to stability in the city, and provide them with protection from possible acts of revenge by the Phalangists" (paragraph 1-a in Exhibit 26). This document cannot be considered a clean warning of the danger of involving the Phalangists in the I.D.F.'s entry into Beirut or an indication of the need to take special precaution in order not to enable the Phalangists to carry out acts of revenge against the Palestinians. In an additional Intelligence document which was issued on 15.9.82 and bears the title "The Murder of Bashir Jemayel—Main Implications," it was said that "the assassination creates conditions for heightening the polarization between the rival Lebanese power elements, for mutual settling of accounts, and for deterioration, which, in the absence of a stabilizing element, is liable to develop into a general civil war" (paragraph 4, Exhibit 25). Neither can this be considered a substantial warning which draws attention to the dangers of acts of revenge by the Phalangists entering West Beirut with the I.D.F. or in its wake.

The director of Military Intelligence said in his testimony that for the issue of sending the Phalangists into the camps to have been discussed and clarified properly, situation-assessment discussions ought to have been held to examine the various topics (which he enumerated in his testimony, p. 1587) connected with the Phalangists' entry into the camps. In his opinion, such a clarification could have been made within a short time; and had it emerged in such a discussion that it were possible to ensure the coordination with—and the command by—the I.D.F. "all the way," he would have supported the entry of the Phalangists, and not the I.D.F., into the camps. We accept these statements of his; but it appears to us that the director of Military Intelligence should have demonstrated sufficient interest in the matter in order to ascertain the role assigned the Phalangists, if for some reason he had not heard about it in the meetings in which he had participated; and it was incumbent upon him to demand that a clarification or discussion be held regarding those topics which he raised in his testimony before us. The fact which the director of Military Intelligence and his representatives point out, namely that the combat morals of the Phalangists and the massacres carried out in the past during the civil war in Lebanon were known to everyone, did not exempt the director of Military Intelligence from the fulfillment of his duties, especially when the issue was cooperation with the Phalangists after the murder of Bashir Jemayel—and this, even if there had not been an organized discussion of this matter.

Less so is there any satisfactory explanation for the lack of substantial action by the director of Military Intelligence in connection with the entry of the Phalangists into the camps, after he had heard on Friday morning not only about the entry of the Phalangists into the camps, but also about the killing of 300 persons in this operation. All he did was give an order to check the veracity of this report, and nothing else. He made no attempt to contact the Chief of Staff or the Defense Minister, to make them aware of the danger in the very operation of the Phalangists in the camps, especially after the receipt of the report of the killing of 300 persons. Indeed, this report was unconfirmed, and he thought that it was from an Operations and not Intelligence source; but it contained information which could have confirmed his fears regarding actions by the Phalangists. In his testimony, the director of Military Intelligence explained why he had made no attempt to warn at that stage of the danger in the situation which had been created. His remarks on this matter are as follows:

"I am labeled as one who has always opposed the Phalangists, not from today, [but] for four years already. In the morning, I read that the Phalangists were inside the camps; and I know that this is as per the Defense Minister's orders—since I have the Duda'i document in hand—and that it is under the command of the I.D.F. So what could I say now? Why do you send it [sic] in without asking me? Or should I act insulted? No, I simply step aside in this matter. That's all."

We believe that in these remarks Major General Saguy revealed the main reason why he "stepped aside" regarding the whole issue; and these remarks of his explain not only his inaction after receiving the report on Friday, but also his behavior at previous stages, as we have described. In our opinion, it was the duty of the director of Military Intelligence, as long as he occupies this post, to demonstrate alertness regarding the role of the Phalangists in the entry into Beirut after Bashir's assassination, to demand an appropriate clarification and to explicitly and expressly warn all those concerned of the expected danger even prior to receipt of the report on Friday, and certainly after receipt of the report. The fear that his words would not receive sufficient attention and be rejected does not justify total inaction. This inaction constitutes breach of the duty incumbent on the director of Military Intelligence in this capacity.

Head of the Institute for Intelligence
and Special Projects (Mossad)
The head of the Mossad was sent a notice under Section 15(A) of the law in which it is stated that he is liable to be harmed if the commission determines that he did not pay appropriate attention to the decision taken regarding the roles to be played by the Phalangists during the I.D.F.'s entry into West Beirut, and did not warn after the murder of Bashir Jemayel of the danger of bloodshed by these forces against the Palestinian population.

The head of the Mossad testified that he first learned of the role given to Phalangists to enter the camps only at the Cabinet meeting on Thursday 16.9.82. On Wednesday, 15.9.82, he received cables from the Mossad representative in Beirut (Exhibits 161 and 162) in which it was reported to him about the meetings of the Chief of Staff and Defense Minister with the Phalangist elite; but in neither of these documents is there any report of the role given the Phalangists in the camps, but rather there is general mention in them that the Phalangists will enter West Beirut after the I.D.F. and will assist the I.D.F. in its operations. In a third cable (Exhibit 163), sent on Thursday at 12:00, it was stated that there had been a coordination meeting with the G.O.C. to prepare the Phalangists "for operations to clear the city of terrorists." In an additional cable sent at that time (Exhibit 164) it was said that the Phalangists would start work at the Burj el-Barajneh camp.

Apparently, the Mossad was not explicitly informed of the Phalangists' entry into the camps, and the head of the Mossad did not know of the decision which had been made on this matter. The testimony of the head of the Mossad should therefore be accepted, that only at the Cabinet meeting of Thursday evening did he hear of the decision regarding the role of the Phalangists and of their entry into the camps, which by then had already taken place.

In the aforementioned circumstances it does not appear to us that the head of the Mossad was obligated, before knowing of the decision regarding the role of the Phalangists, to offer at his initiative an assessment regarding the situation which was liable to develop if the Phalangists would be given the opportunity to take revenge on the Palestinians and attempt to carry out their plans for them in West Beirut. The head of the Mossad was present at the Cabinet meeting until its conclusion. He heard what was said there, but did not himself give a situation assessment regarding the entry of the Phalangists into the camps, and did not express any reservation about this entry. He spoke at that meeting about the Mossad's assessment regarding the situation created after the murder of Bashir, but his remarks did not explicitly deal with the issue of the Phalangists' entry into the camps or with the problems which could ensue therefrom. A certain hint of the danger of irregular actions by the Phalangists can be found in the following remarks made by the head of the Mossad at that meeting (p. 26 in Exhibit 122):

"When we learned of the death of Bashir—and this was close to midnight—we thought that there could be two phenomena: one, that the whole forest would catch fire, and the Phalangist forces themselves, which were suddenly left without a commander, [and] with a desire for revenge, could also have taken uncontrolled action; and on the other hand, those Palestinians and Lebanese organizations which were in West Beirut, suddenly learning that the leader of the Phalangists was dead and knowing that the Phalangists may well have been weakened as a result, it was possible that they would start up—i.e., there was definitely the possibility that a situation of total conflagration would flare up in the city."

These remarks should not be considered an unequivocal warning of the danger entailed in the entry of the Phalangists into the camps, an entry about which the head of the Mossad made no comment in the situation assessment which he gave at the Cabinet meeting. The head of the Mossad did not express any reservation about the entry of the

Phalangists into the camps. In his first testimony he said that had he been asked at that meeting about the entry of the Phalangists into the camps, he would have recommended this "with the warning that they not carry out a massacre" and with the belief that such a warning would be effective—and this, according to the Mossad's experience with certain operations carried out together with the Phalangists in the past (p. 173). In his additional testimony, the head of the Mossad said that the data which the Mossad had at the time of the Cabinet meeting did not indicate and did not warn of the possibility of atrocities in the camps.

The data which he presented (p. 1428) were that according to the reports received, despite the murder of Bashir, the military commander of the Phalangists was in control of his forces; and in addition, according to the information which the Mossad had, the murder of Bashir was carried out not by the Palestinians but by the Mourabitoun. This last argument is far from convincing. It is not at all certain that the Phalangists knew at that time who carried out the assassination; and even if they had known this, it is most doubtful whether this would have moderated their actions against the Palestinians, whom they considered the source of all the tragedies which had befallen Lebanon, and who had cooperated with the Mourabitoun in the fighting against the Phalangists.

The question is whether this inaction by the head of the Mossad constitutes breach of a duty incumbent upon the head of the Mossad.

The answer to this question is not easy. As mentioned above, the view of the Mossad, which had ben expressed for a fairly long period prior to the I.D.F.'s entry into Lebanon, as well as afterwards, was that there should be greater cooperation with the Phalangists. The view prevalent in the Mossad, as expressed in various documents, was that the Phalangists are a trustworthy element which can be relied upon, and this despite the Phalangists' past regarding their attitude to the Palestinians and their statements on the way to solve the Palestinian problem once they reach power. The head of the Mossad himself noted in part of his testimony mentioned above, that this approach of the Mossad was influenced by the development of subjective feelings by representatives of the Mossad, who were in constant contact with the leaders of the Phalangists. We do not believe that the head of the Mossad can be held responsible for the existence of such a "conception." He assumed the position of head of the Mossad only on 12.9.82—that is, two days before the murder of Bashir. He had previously been the deputy head of the Mossad and was acquainted with the Mossad's affairs; but the responsibility for the way in which the Mossad operated was not his. The entry of the Phalangists into the camps did not contradict the Mossad's situation assessment; and therefore it is difficult to expect that the head of the Mossad would have reservations about this decision when he heard about it at the Cabinet meeting on 16.9.82. In this matter as well, it should be taken into account that he had then been serving as head of the Mossad for only four days, and that this was the first Cabinet meeting in which he participated in this capacity.

It appears to us, that even in the situation described above, the head of the Mossad was obligated to express his opinion at the Cabinet meeting on the entry of the Phalangists and deal in this expression of opinion with the dangers involved in the Phalangists' operations—especially after he had heard Minister David Levy's remarks. In consideration of all the aforementioned circumstances, it is our opinion that this inaction of the head of the Mossad should not be considered serious.

G.O.C. Northern Command,
Major General Amir Drori

In the notification sent to G.O.C. Northern Command, Amir Drori, it was stated that he is liable to be harmed if the commission determines that he did not take appropriate or sufficient steps to prevent the continuation of the Phalangists' actions in the refugee camps when he received reports of acts of killing or acts which deviate from regular combat operations which were carried out in the camps.

On Thursday night, the division Intelligence officer transmitted the report of 300 killed to the Northern Command, but this report did not reach Major General Drori and he did not hear a thing about what was happening in the camps until Friday morning.

We have enumerated above the differences between the versions of Major General Drori and Brigadier General Yaron regarding the circumstances surrounding Major Drori's visit to the forward command post, the conversation which preceded this visit, and the conversation which took place during the visit. According to the testimony of Major General Drori, the visit was made at his initiative, without his knowing that any problem had arisen regarding the camps, while according to Brigadier General Yaron's version, Major General Drori's appearance was the result of a conversation in which Brigadier General Yaron reported his uneasy feelings regarding what was being done in the camps. We do not find that the differing versions on this subject are important in the matter before us.

Neither was there a uniform version regarding the reports transmitted to Major General Drori during his meeting at the forward command post. Colonel Duvdevani said in his statement that he had told Major General Drori about 100 killed in the Phalangists' operations; while according to Major General Drori's testimony, he did not hear in this visit about killing in the camps or about a specific number of killed. From Brigadier General Yaron's remarks it is apparent that he did not report to Major General Drori about the reports of the 300 killed and the 45 persons who had been captured by the Phalangists, since he had thought that these reports were unsubstantiated. Regarding the things Major General Drori heard from Brigadier General Yaron, Major General Drori's version differs only in unimportant details from Brigadier General Yaron's version. It appears to us that it is not possible to determine with sufficient certainty that clear reports were given to Major General Drori about killing in the camps. We believe, however, that in his testimony before us, Major General Drori belittled the importance and significance of the things about which he had heard in the meeting at the forward command post, as well as the impression these had made on him. It should be noted that Major General Drori was aware that the Phalangists were liable to act in an uncontrolled way, and this not necessarily from his conversation with an officer connected with the Lebanese Army on Thursday evening, but mainly from his knowledge of the Phalangists, based on his constant contact with them. There is therefore no room for doubt that after the conversations which he held on the roof of the forward command post on Friday morning, he was aware that the continuation of the Phalangists' actions in the refugee camps posed danger. Three actions which he took are evidence of this. The first—the order he gave regarding cessation of the Phalangists' actions; the second—a telephone report to the Chief of Staff that the Phalangists "had overdone it" and that he had ordered their operation stopped; and the third—the continuation of his efforts to impress upon the commander of the Lebanese Army that this army enter the camps instead of the Phalangists. Here we should mention that in this persuasion effort, Major General Drori told the commander of the Lebanese Army, "You know what the Lebanese are capable of doing to each other." These remarks, in the context in which they were made, in a section of Major General Drori's testimony as cited above, show that Major General Drori had realized the gravity of the matter and the need to make efforts to terminate the Phalangists' operations in the camps.

Taking into consideration that it has not been proved that Major General Drori had [received] explicit reports about acts of killing and about their extent, it appears to us that he acted properly, wisely, and responsibly, with sufficient alertness at this stage. He heard from the Chief of Staff that the latter was to arrive in Beirut in the afternoon hours and could rely on the fact that this visit by the Chief of Staff, which was to take place within a few hours, would lead to positive results regarding the Phalangists' activity in the camps.

In the notification as per Section 15(A) of the law, Major General Drori was informed that he is liable to be harmed if it is determined that he did not warn the Chief of Staff when the latter arrived in Beirut on 17.9.82 of the danger posed to the population in the camps from the continued activity or continued presence of the Phalangists in the camps, and did not try—at a meeting with the Phalangist commanders, or shortly thereafter—to prevent the continuation of such activity.

According to the testimony of Major General Drori, it was clear that he was satisfied with an absolutely passive role regarding the issue of the Phalangists in the camps, from the time the Chief of Staff arrived in Beirut and later. Major General Drori did not emphasize to the Chief of Staff before the meeting with the Phalangist commanders that it was necessary to end the Phalangists' presence in the camps or take some kind of action which could ensure that the Phalangists' actions against the non-combatant populace would stop. This refraining from bringing the importance and seriousness of the matter to the attention of the Chief of Staff was explained by Major General Drori by the fact that after the meeting on the roof of the foward command post with Brigadier General Yaron, the acuteness of his sense of imminent danger diminished, for two reasons. The first reason was that a few hours had gone by before the Chief of Staff arrived, and no additional reports had come in. The second reason which calmed Major General Drori was that at his meeting with the commander of the Lebanese Army, he had not heard anything about irregular occurrences in the camps, despite the fact that the Lebanese Army was deployed around the camps, including at the places where the Phalangists had entered, and Lebanese Army personnel should have known if something unusual had happened in the camps (Major General Drori's testimony, pp. 1611-1615).

These reasons for the diminished sense of the matter's importance are not convincing. It is difficult to consider the lack of additional reports a calming factor, when only a few hours are involved and when Major General Drori made no special efforts, while on the roof of the forward command post and while speaking with the officers there, to investigate and testify the details of the reports reaching him, and did not give orders to conduct special checks on what was going on in the camps. He also did not speak during the meeting on the roof of the forward command post with the Phalangists' liaison officer, who was present there. At the meeting with the commander of the Lebanese Army, Major General Drori did not ask whether the commander had any reports on events in the camps, but drew his conclusion which reduced his alertness solely from the fact that his commander did not "volunteer" any information.

We described above what happened at the meeting with the Phalangist commanders, in which the subject of the Phalangist forces' behavior in the camps did not come up at all. In our opinion, even though the Chief of Staff conducted the meeting for the Israeli side, it was Major General Drori's duty to at least make an attempt to raise the issue at this meeting. He also made no attempt to persuade the Chief of Staff to raise the matter at the meeting with the Phalangists, but was satisfied with sitting idly by. Major General Drori is a senior commander with a very important task, who bears heavy responsibility for events on a wide front. A commander at such a level and rank should be expected to take the initiative when he sees that the Chief of Staff does not intend to deal with the issue which was the main cause of his coming to Beirut and holding a meeting with the Phalangist staff. If this passive behavior by Major General Drori was the result of a significant decline in his alertness during the time which had gone by since ordering a halt to the Phalangists' operations, then we have already said above that this reduced alertness was not at all justified. Also, after the conclusion of the meeting with the Phalangist commanders, Major General Drori did nothing about the behavior of the Phalangists and did not raise the matter for discussion with the Chief of Staff. The Phalangist's request that the I.D.F. supply them with tractors should have increased the suspicion that actions which are difficult to describe as combat operations were being carried out in the camps; and apparently this suspicion arose, since the order was to provide the Phalangists with only one tractor and remove the I.D.F. markings from it. We cannot find justification for Major General Drori's disengagement from any treatment of the subject of Phalangist behavior, from the moment the Chief of Staff arrived in Beirut and until after the departure of the Phalangists from the camps.

We determine that it was the duty of the G.O.C. to warn the Chief of Staff, when the latter arrived in Beirut on 17.9.82 and during the rest of the Chief of Staff's stay in Beirut, that the population in the camps is endangered by the continued presence of the Phalangist forces in the camps and that they should be removed from there immediately—or that at least steps be taken to ensure the safety of the population in the camps or to reduce the danger they face to the barest possible minimum. Major General Drori's refraining from any action regarding the danger facing the civilian population from the Phalangist forces, from the time the Chief of Staff arrived in Beirut and until Saturday, 18.9.82, constitutes, in our opinion, a breach of the duty which was incumbent on Major General Drori.

Division Commander Brig-
adier, General Amos Yaron

The first issue specified in the notice sent to Brigadier General Amos Yaron under Section 15(A) of the law is that Brigadier General Yaron did not properly evaluate and did not check reports that reached him concerning acts of killing and other irregular actions of the Phalangists in the camps, did not pass on that information to the G.O.C. and to the Chief of Staff immediately after it had been received on 16.9.82, and did not take the appropriate steps to stop the Phalangists' actions and to protect the population in the camps immediately upon receiving the reports.

We determined in the specification of the facts that Brigadier General Yaron received reports of acts of killing in the evening and night hours of 16.9.82. He received the first report from Lieutenant Elul, and from it it should have been clear to him that the Phalangists were killing women and children in the camps. Brigadier General Yaron heard an additional report that same evening from the division Intelligence officer concerning the fate of the group of 45 people who were in the Phalangists' hands. A third report was delivered by the Phalangists' liaison officer, G., about 300 killed, a number which was later reduced to 120. Even if we suppose that the first and second reports were considered by Brigadier General Yaron to be about the same event, nevertheless, from all the reports, it became known to Brigadier General Yaron that the Phalangists were perpetrating acts of killing which went beyond combat operations, and were killing women and children as well. That evening he was satisfied with reiterating the warnings to the Phalangists' liaison officer and to Elie Hobeika not to kill women and children; but beyond that he did nothing to stop the killing. He did not pass on the information that he had received to Major General Drori that evening nor on the following day in the morning call, nor when they met before noon. When Brigadier General Yaron heard from the division Intelligence officer, in the briefing on 16.9.82, about the report indicating the danger that women and children were being killed, he interrupted him—and it appears from the transcript of the conversation that took place then that Brigadier General Yaron wished to play down the importance of the matter and to cut off the clarification of the issue at that briefing. Brigadier General Yaron testified that he was, indeed, aware that the Phalangists' norms of behavior during wartime are different from those of the I.D.F. and that there is no sense in arguing with them to change their combat ethics; but since in previous Phalangist operations conducted jointly with the I.D.F. they had not behaved aberrantly, he trusted that his reiterated warnings not to kill women and children would suffice, the Phalangist commanders' promises would be kept, and the steps that he had taken in order to obtain information on the Phalangists' operations would enable him to follow their actions. We are not prepared to accept this explanation. We have already determined that the means of supervision over what the Phalangists were doing in the camps could not ensure the flow of real and immediate information on their actions. It is difficult to understand how Brigadier General Yaron relied on these warnings and assurances, when he knew about the Phalangists' combat ethics. He also did not take into account the influence of the assassination of Bashir on the fanning of the Phalangists' feelings of revenge. Already shortly after the Phalangists' entrance into the camps, he started receiving reports which should have clarified to him the gravity of the danger of a massacre being perpetrated in the camps and which should have spurred him to take immediate steps, whether on his own cognizance or by authorization from the G.O.C. or the Chief of Staff, to prevent the continuation of operations of these kinds. No action was taken by Brigadier General Yaron, and neither did he see to conveying the information in his possession to his superiors.

An additional explanation by which Brigadier General Yaron tried to justify his behavior was that in the situation which existed that night, the reports about 300, or fewer, killed did not seem to him sufficiently important to spur him to check whether they were true, since on that night, in his role as division commander, he had combat problems which were much more important than the matter of the Phalangists in the camps (testimony of Brigadier General Yaron on p. 699). We cannot accept this explanation either. If Brigadier General Yaron could find the time to hold a briefing, he could also have issued orders to pass on the reports and to take appropriate measures such as were called for by the information received.

Perhaps it is possible to find an explanation for Brigadier General Yaron's refraining from any substantial reaction to the serious information which had reached him Thursday evening in that he was interested that the Phalangists continue to operate in the camps so that I.D.F. soldiers would not have to engage in fighting in that area. Brigadier General Yaron had no reservations about admitting the Phalangists into the camps; he testified that he was happy with this decision and explained his position in that "we have been fighting here for four months already and there is a place where they can take part in the fighting, the fighting serves their purposes as well, so let them participate and not let the I.D.F. do everything" (p.695). It is possible to show understanding for this feeling, but it does not justify a lack of any action on the part of Brigadier General Yaron, considering the reports that had reached him.

During Friday as well, Brigadier General Yaron did not act properly with regard to the Phalangist operation in the camps. When he met with Major General Drori, he was obligated to report all the information that had reached him, but he did not do so. As a result of this failure, Major General Drori was not apprised of all the information that had reached the division by that time. A number of times, Brigadier General Yaron approached the Phalangist officers who were at the forward command post, including Elie Hobeika, and repeated the admonition not to do harm to women and children; but other than this he did not take any initiative and only suggested that the Phalangists be ordered not to advance—and an order to this effect was issued by Major General Drori. This order might have been regarded as enough of a precaution by Major General Drori, who had not heard about instances of killing; but Brigadier General Yaron should have known that halting the advance did not ensure an end to the killing.

The notice sent to Brigadier General Yaron under Section 15(A) also speaks of the failure to provide any warning to the Chief of Staff when the latter reached Beirut on 17.9.82, as well as of Brigadier General Yaron's granting the Phalangists permission to send a new force into the camps without taking any steps that would bring a stop to the excesses. When the Chief of Staff came to Beirut Brigadier General Yaron did not tell him everything he had heard and did not make any suggestion to him about the continuation of the Phalangist operation in the camps. From the time he saw the Chief of Staff (after his arrival in Beirut) until the Chief of Staff left Beirut, no warning was heard from Brigadier General Yaron—not even a significant comment regarding the danger of a massacre. Brigadier General Yaron was not oblivious to this danger. We have evidence that on Friday he had spoken to the Phalangist liaison officer charging that his men were killing women and children (statement no. 23 by Colonel Agmon), but he did not express this awareness clearly in his meetings with Major General Drori and the Chief of Staff.

Brigadier General Yaron's inaction regarding the continuation of the Phalangist operation in the camps was epitomized by the fact that he did not issue any order to prevent them from replacing forces on Friday and did not impose any supervision on the movement of the Phalangist forces to and from the camps, despite the fact that the order halting the operation was not rescinded.

We have already cited Brigadier General Yaron's statement at the Senior Command Meeting in which he admitted with laudable candor that this was an instance of "insensitivity" on his part and on the part of others concerned. As we have already stated above, Brigadier General Yaron's desire was to save I.D.F. soldiers from having to carry out the operation in the camps, and this appears to be the main reason for his insensitivity to the dangers of the massacre in the camps. This concern of a commander for the welfare of his men would be praiseworthy in other circumstances; but considering the state of affairs in this particular instance, it was a thoroughly mistaken judgment on the part of Brigadier General Yaron, and a grave error was commited by a high-ranking officer of an I.D.F. force in this sector.

We determine that by virtue of his failings and his actions, detailed above, Brigadier General Yaron committed a breach of the duties incumbent upon him by virtue of his position.

Mr. Avi Duda'i, Personal Aide
to the Minister of Defense
The sole issue regarding which the notice was sent to Mr. Duda'i was "that on 17.9.82, during the morning hours or before noon, Mr. Duda'i received a report about killings that had been perpetrated by the Lebanese forces in the refugee camps, and did not pass this report on to the Minister of Defense."

In his testimony, Mr. Duda'i denied that any report on what was happening in the camps was given to him on 17.9.82. Yet Lieutenant Colonel Gai, an officer in the National Security Unit, testified before us that on Friday morning, 17.9.82, he was in the office of the director of Military Intelligence, where he met one of the officers who works in the office, Captain Moshe Sinai, who told him (according to Lt. Col. Gai) "as a piece of gossip" that about 300 persons had been killed in the camps in Beirut, and that, at around 11:00-11:30 that same day, he—Lt. Col. Gai—in one of his telephone conversations with Duda'i, told Duda'i what he had heard from Captain Sinai (testimony by Gai, pp. 921-923). In his second round of testimony, too, Gai stood by his story that he had passed this report on to Duda'i; except that according to this testimony, the report was not given at about 11:00 but rather at a later hour, between 12:30—when Duda'i arrived at the Foreign Ministry, whence he spoke with Gai—and 15:00 hours.

Lieutenant Colonel Hevroni, bureau chief to the director of Military Intelligence, testified that he had been with Duda'i at the Sde Dov airfield for a meeting that the Defense Minister had summoned there, [and] afterwards had come to Jerusalem with Duda'i for a meeting at the Foreign Minister's office which had lasted until 15:00 hours; and during that same period of time, Duda'i asked him what was happening regarding Gai's and Sinai's story—and the reply was that there was no verification of this report. It was clear to Hevroni from this conversation that Duda'i had gotten the report which Gai had received from Sinai (testimony of Hevroni, pp. 876-877). We also heard additional testimony which was intended to show that, post factum, Duda'i admitted, in the presence of Gai and the witness Colonel Kniazher (called Zizi), that Gai had told him about the report on Friday; but from Colonel Kniazher's testimony (pp. 1466-1468) it turns out that Gai wasn't present at the time he spoke with Duda'i, and Duda'i wasn't present at the time that Kniazher spoke with Gai. (p. 1466); and there is no evidence in Kniazher's testimony that Duda'i had heard about the report from Gai on 17.9.82.

As has been said, an investigation was held in the director of Military Intelligence's bureau after the event, as a result of which an investigative report was drawn up (Exhibit 29). In paragraph 6 of this report, it is stated that the visit by Lt. Col. Gai between the hours of 7:30-8:00 was intended to clarify what had happened to two Military Intelligence documents which had not yet reached the Defense Minister.

From the testimonies we have heard, it becomes apparent that Gai's visit in the morning hours was for the purpose of receiving reports from Military Intelligence about that attack on the tank which had occurred in West Beirut. Gai did pay two visits to the director of Military Intelligence's bureau that same day, but this second visit was at about 11:00 hours and was carried out on an order that Duda'i transmitted by phone from Sde Dov to Gai, so that the latter would clarify the matter of the documents. This inaccuracy would indeed appear tiny, but it has a certain significance in that it fits in with testimonies that on that same Friday morning, Duda'i complained to those who work in his office, including Gai, that there were defects in the reporting of what was happening in Lebanon and that reports weren't reaching the Defense Ministry. Here it should be noted that on that same day, the Defense Minister's military adjutant was not in the office because he was on vacation, and Duda'i was taking his place.

In paragraph 13 of Exhibit 29, it is said that "in retrospect (in reconstruction) it turned out that Lt. Col. Gai—after receiving the report from the bureau chief of the director of Military Intelligence—looked into the matter on the morning of 17 September with Operations Branch, after he, too, had gotten the impression that an Operations report/occurrence was at issue; and in the investigation, he was told that Operations did not know about such an action by the Phalangists." In his testimony, Gai said that these statements were inaccurate, and that he had only inquired at operations if there was anything new from Beirut and had received a negative reply. In paragraph 14 of Exhibit 29, it is said that "in a second update between minister's aide Avi Duda'i and Lt. Col. Gai, Duda'i reported that he had spoken with the bureau chief of the director of Military Intelligence, who had told him that the report had not received verification from Military Intelligence personnel who had looked into the matter." What is said here was not confirmed by Lt. Col. Gai's testimony; and as mentioned, Duda'i denied receiving any report. The rather obvious general trend of Exhibit 29 regarding the report to Gai is: to show that report on the contents of the cable on the 300 killed was conveyed from the director of Military Intelligence's bureau to the Defense Minister's bureau. According to Lt. Col. Gai's testimony, the conversation between him and Captain Sinai cannot be viewed as more than "an exchange of gossip," and it is difficult to treat such a conversation as a proper act of conveying an important report.

Captain Sinai gave a statement to the staff investigators (no. 112) in which he said that he had read the cable (Appendix A, Exhibit 29) in front of Lt. Col. Gai, and that the latter had reacted to it with the words, "Listen, that's very interesting"—and, as far as Sinai recalls, he said, "I spoke with the minister during the night, and I'll go talk with him in a little while; the story is very interesting, and the minister will be very happy to hear the report." According to Sinai, this is more or less the version he heard from Gai. We find it difficult to attribute importance to this statement. In his statement, Sinai gave exact details concerning a seach for the two documents which preceded the conversation between Gai and himself, and at present it is already clear that he erred in this, because the search for the documents was not conducted in the early hours of the morning, but rather close to the noon hour. It is not reasonable [to suppose that] if Gai did indeed receive Sinai's report as an interesting or important report, he would not immediately convey it to Duda'i, who on that same morning complained several times about a lack of reporting on what was happening in Lebanon and inquired after such reports from time to time.

It is our opinion that it cannot be determined that Gai did indeed pass on the contents of the above report to Duda'i on Friday. The doubt stems not only from contradictions revealed in the witnesses' statements, but also from [the fact] that the witnesses who told about the conveying of the report have an interest in showing that they fulfilled their obligation in transmitting the report from the director of Military Intelligence's bureau to the Defense Minister's aide. It is also difficult to treat Gai's testimony as testimony by someone who is a disinterested party in the matter, since it is in his interest to show, after all that happened, that he did not keep the contents of the report he'd heard from Sinai to himself. Gai also did not give a satisfactory explanation as to why, according to his version, he had told Duda'i about this report only in the afternoon, despite the fact that Duda'i was constantly asking whether reports had come in from Lebanon and was complaining about a lack of reports. In view of the entire body of evidence, we do not determine that Duda'i indeed received the report about the 300 people killed on Friday, 17.9.82, and it therefore cannot be determined that he refrained from fulfilling an obligation which was incumbent upon him, as was stated in the notice of [possible] harm which was sent to him.

THE FUNCTIONING
OF ESTABLISHMENTS

Thus far we have dealt with the findings and conclusions regarding the course of events, and the responsibility for them of those persons whose actions had a decisive effect on the course of events. As we noted, we decided not to discuss the activities of other persons who were close to the course of events but who played a secondary role. All these persons, whether they had central or secondary roles, operated within organizational frameworks whose functioning was flawed.

In this section of the report we wish to dwell briefly on the flaws in the functioning of these organizational establishments. We shall devote only a few comments to this important topic, with the aim of pointing to a number of flaws which seem to us worrisome, and to bring about a situation in which all the responsible authorities—civil and military— will take all the requisite measures so that the reasons and causes for these flaws will be examined and analyzed, the lessons therefrom learned, and so that what requires amending will indeed be amended. As in this entire report, we shall deal only with the functioning of the various establishments from the time the decision was taken on the entry of the Phalangists into the camps until their departure. Within this framework, too, we shall offer our opinion only regarding outstanding matters which are especially noteworthy. Unquestionably, there were many establishments that functioned properly, even excellently; but in the nature of things our attention is directed toward those establishments in which were revealed flaws that are relevant to the subject of the commission's scrutiny. Hence, the major part of our attention is directed to two key topics which concern us: one is the flaws in the course of decision-taking by the policy-making institutions; the other is the flaws in the manner of handling the information which was received.

The decision on the entry of the Phalangists into the refugee camps was taken on Wednesday (15.9.82) in the morning. The Prime Minister was not then informed of the decision. The Prime Minister heard about the decision, together with all the other ministers, in the course of a report made by the Chief of Staff at the Cabinet session on Thursday (16.9.82) when the Phalangists were already in the camps. Thereafter, no report was made to the Prime Minister regarding the excesses of the Phalangists in the camps, and the Prime Minister learned about the events in the camps from a BBC broadcast on Saturday (18.9.82) afternoon. This state of affairs is unsatisfactory on two planes: first, the importance of the decision on the entry of the Phalangists, against the backdrop of the Lebanese situation as it was known to those concerned, required that the decision on having the Phalangists enter the camps be made with the prior approval of the Prime Minister. Moreover, once the decision had been taken without the Prime Minister's participation, orderly processes of government required that the decision be made known to him at the earliest possible moment. It is not proper procedure for the Prime Minister to hear about this decision in an incidental manner along with the other Cabinet ministers during a Cabinet session, when the Phalangists were already in the camps.

Second, once the decision was taken, orderly processes of government required that the Prime Minister be informed of any excesses committed. What the Defense Minister, the Chief of Staff and the General of Command knew on Friday and on Saturday morning, the Prime Minister ought also to have known. It is inconceivable that the Prime Minister should receive his information about this from a foreign radio station.

As we have seen, the decision on the Phalangists' entry into the camps took final shape on Wednesday morning (15.9.82) on the roof of the divisional forward command post. When this decision was taken its ramifications were not examined, nor were its advantages and disadvantages weighed. This is explicable in that the decision was taken under pressure of time. Nonetheless, enough time existed before the Phalangists' entry on Thursday evening (16.9.82) to carry out a situation appraisal in which the decision, its manner of execution, and its possible results could be examined. No such deliberation in fact took place. The discussion held by the Defense Minister on Thursday morning (Exhibit 27), in which he said, "I would move the Phalangists into the camps," cannot be regarded as a situation appraisal in the usual sense of the term. The Chief of Staff told us that on Wednesday he ordered his deputy to hold a consultation among branch heads. Such a discussion did in fact take place in the late afternoon hours (Exhibit 130), but it was a briefing and not a situation appraisal. The issue of the Phalangists' entry was mentioned in that discussion in a general manner, but the decision was not presented in detail, no examination was made of the security measures to be taken, and no evaluation was made of the possible ramifications of the decision.

The way in which decisions are to be taken and the appropriate bodies to that end have been laid down in the procedures. These formats ought to be exploited in order to enhance the prospect that when decisions are taken, all the information at hand, the various positions, the pros and cons, and the possible ramifications of the decision will be taken into account.

Experience and intuition are very valuable, but it is preferable that they not constitute the sole basis on which decisions are taken.

The absence of the required staff discussion regarding the entry of the Phalangists into the camps was accompanied by another inevitable flaw. The information about the decision was not transmitted in an orderly fashion to all the parties who should have known about it. We have already seen that the Prime Minister was unaware of the decision. The Foreign Minister, too, learned of the Phalangists' entry only in the Cabinet session. We have already cited the account of the director of Military Intelligence that he, too, did not learn about the decision until Friday morning. Although we have stated that we find it difficult to accept that account, this cannot justify the absence of an orderly report about the decision being made to all the various staff elements.

Thus, for example, it emerged that the Command Intelligence officers were first briefed by the Command Intelligence Officer about the fact that the Phalangists would enter the camps on Thrusday, some two hours after the operation had already commenced. According to the testimony of the Military Intelligence / Research officers whose task it is to prepare situation appraisals, they received no prior information about the decision to have the Phalangists enter the camps.

As a result, that department was unable to prepare its own appraisals, as would have been expected of it prior to the Phalangists' entry into the camps. This also had a certain effect on the manner in which that department functioned at the stage when it received the report about the 300 killed (Section 6, Appendix B).

The head of the Mossad learned of the decision only at the Cabinet session. Despite the fact that Mossad personnel were in Beirut when the events occurred and maintained ongoing contacts with the Phalangist commanders, no report was received from them regarding the special role of the Phalangists in the camps prior to their entry, nor did they collect any data at all on events in the camps after the Phalangists had entered.

This is not a satisfactory state of affairs. Orderly processes required that the decision on the entry of the Phalangists be reported in an orderly and documented manner to the various bodies that should know about it, so that they could direct their activities accordingly.

The military establishments are based, inter alia, on diverse channels of reporting. An examination of the events on the dates relevant here indicates the existence of considerable flaws in these channels of reporting. Matters that should have been reported were not reported at all, or were reported late and in fragmentary fashion. For example, the report about the behavior of the Phalangists in the field was not transmitted to

Divisional Intelligence. For its part, the latter did not relay the reports about the 45 civilians—which was brought to its attention already on Thursday evening—to Command Intelligence. As for Command Intelligence, despite the fact that it received a report from the division regarding the 300 killed, it did not convey it to General Staff/Military Intelligence. The transmission of the report to Military Intelligence was the result of the fine initiative of Intelligence Officer A.

We find a similar picture also in the Operations Branch channels. Operations Branch Command did not receive an orderly report of what was happening in the field. As we have seen, already on Thursday evening and Friday morning—and throughout Friday—reports were collected by a considerable number of soldiers and officers who were near the camps. Only some of those reports—and those in fragmentary fashion—were brought to the attention of the Divisional Operations elements. Divisional Operations for its part did not relay the information it had in an orderly fashion to Command Operations elements. Thus, for example, the reports in the possession of Divisional Operations about the 300 killed (or the 120 killed) were not transmitted at all to Command Operations. The latter did not report (not even on the actual entry of the Phalangists into the camps) to Operations Branch/Operations. Thus, for example, the report about the 300 killed was received already on Thursday evening in Command Intelligence. For some reason that report was not conveyed (neither in its telephone form nor in the form of the subsequent cable) to the knowledge of the Command Intelligence Officer. The report was not transmitted to Command Operations, and *ipso facto* was not brought to the knowledge of the G.O.C., either that evening or the following day. Similarly, no orderly report was made regarding the decision of the G.O.C. Northern Command about halting the operations of the Phalangists. These flaws in the reporting require examination and analysis, since in the absence of an orderly and proper report the decision-makers at the various levels lack the information required for their decisions.

The reports that were received via the various channels were also not always handled according to the standing procedures, the result being that the reports sometimes became worthless. Sometimes, reports received were not recorded in the designated log books; reports that were relayed were sometimes transmitted with important omissions, which prevented their being handled properly. Reports that were dealt with (such as the handling of the report about the 300 killed within the framework of Military Intelligence/Research) were at times handled superficially, with a fruitless internal runaround and without exhausting the various possibilities for verification and examination. Other Intelligence means employed sometimes failed to produce the information that was expected of them (see Section 5, Appendix B). Reports that were received and which required a preliminary evaluation to determine their significance and possible implications were not dealt with properly and in the meantime were rendered worthless due to a protracted process of examining their authenticity.

In the course of the testimony we heard, we often came across conversations—whether face-to-face or over the telephone or radio—between highly responsible personnel. Contradictions were often evident in the testimony about these conversations—not out of any intention to conceal the truth, but as a natural result of flaws in human memory. There is no satisfactory explanation of why no notes were taken of these conversations. The Prime Minister held many conversations with the Defense Minister and the Chief of Staff, including the conversations in which the decision was taken to seize key positions in West Beirut. It is not surprising, therefore, if a certain difference exists between the Prime Minister's version of a guideline issued by him and that of the Chief of Staff regarding the guideline he received.

The Defense Minister and the Chief of Staff held a conversation on Tuesday evening in which a number of important decisions were taken. This conversation was not recorded in any form.

We believe that it is desirable to determine guidelines in this matter in order to prevent a situation in which important decisions are not documented. Precisely because human memory is often faulty, it is desirable to determine a proper method and procedure for recording those conversations which, according to criteria to be determined, it is important to keep on record.

RECOMMENDATIONS

With regard to the following recommendations concerning a group of men who hold senior positions in the Government and the Israel Defense Forces, we have taken into account [the fact] that each one of these men has to his credit [the performance of] many public or military services rendered with sacrifice and devotion on behalf of the State of Israel. If nevertheless we have reached the conclusion that it is incumbent upon us to recommend certain measures against some of these men, it is out of the recognition that the gravity of the matter and its implications for the underpinnings of public morality in the State of Israel call for such measures.

The Prime Minister, The Foreign Minister, and the Head of the Mossad

We have heretofore established the facts and conclusions with regard to the responsibility of the Prime Minister, the Foreign Minister, and the head of the Mossad. In view of what we have determined with regard to the extent of the responsibility of each of them, we are of the opinion that it is sufficient to determine responsibility and there is no need for any further recommendations.

G.O.C. Northern Command, Major General Amir Drori

We have detailed above our conclusions with regard to the responsibility of G.O.C. Northern Command Major General Amir Drori. Major General Drori was charged with many difficult and complicated tasks during the week the I.D.F. entered West Beirut, missions which he had to accomplish after a long period of difficult warfare. He took certain measures for terminating the Phalangists' actions, and his guilt lies in that he did not continue with these actions. Taking into account these circumstances, it appears to us that it is sufficient to determine the responsibility of Major General Drori without recourse to any further recommendation.

The Minister of Defense, Mr. Ariel Sharon

We have found, as has been detailed in this report, that the Minister of Defense bears personal responsibility. In our opinion, it is fitting that the Minister of Defense draw the appropriate personal conclusions arising out of the defects revealed with regard to the manner in which he discharged the duties of his office—and if necessary, that the Prime Minister consider whether he should exercise his authority under Section 21-A(a) of the Basic Law of the Government, according to which "the Prime Minister may, after informing the Cabinet of his intention to do so, remove a minister from office."

The Chief of Staff, Lt.-Gen. Rafael Eitan

We have arrived at grave conclusions with regard to the acts and omissions of the Chief of Staff, Lt.-Gen. Rafael Eitan. The Chief of Staff is about to complete his term of service in April, 1983. Taking into account the fact that an extension of his term is not under consideration, there is no [practical] significance to a recommendation with regard to his continuing in office as Chief of Staff, and therefore we have resolved that it is sufficient to determine responsibility without making any further recommendation.

The Director of Military Intelligence,
Major General Yehoshua Saguy

We have detailed the various extremely serious omissions of the director of Military Intelligence, Major General Yehoshua Saguy, in discharging the duties of his office. We recommend that Major General Yehoshua Saguy not continue as director of Military Intelligence.

Division Commander, Brigadier
General Amos Yaron

We have detailed above the extent of the responsibility of Brigadier General Amos Yaron. Taking into account all the circumstances, we recommend that Brigadier General Amos Yaron not serve in the capacity of a field commander in the Israel Defense Forces, and that this recommendation not be reconsidered before three years have passed.

In the course of this inquiry, shortcomings in the functioning of [several] establishments have been revealed, as described in the chapter dealing with this issue. One must learn the appropriate lessons from these shortcomings, and we recommend that, in addition to internal control in this matter, an investigation into the shortcomings and the manner of correcting them be undertaken by an expert or experts, to be appointed by a Ministerial Defense Committee. If in the course of this investigation it be found that certain persons bear responsibility for these shortcomings, it is fitting that the appropriate conclusions be drawn in their regard, whether in accordance with the appropriate provisions of the military legal code, or in some other manner.

CLOSING REMARKS

In the witnesses' testimony and in various documents, stress is laid on the difference between the usual battle ethics of the I.D.F. and the battle ethics of the bloody clashes and combat actions among the various ethnic groups, militias, and fighting forces in Lebanon. The difference is considerable. In the war the I.D.F. waged in Lebanon, many civilians were injured and much loss of life was caused, despite the effort the I.D.F. and its soldiers made not to harm civilians. On more than one occasion, this effort caused I.D.F. troops additional casualties. During the months of the war, I.D.F. soldiers witnessed many sights of killing, destruction, and ruin. From their reactions (about which we have heard) to acts of brutality against civilians, it would appear that despite the terrible sights and experiences of the war and despite the soldier's obligation to behave as a fighter with a certain degree of callousness, I.D.F. soldiers did not lose their sensitivity to atrocities that were perpetrated on noncombatants either out of cruelty or to give vent to vengeful feelings. It is regrettable that the reaction by I.D.F. soldiers to such deeds was not always forceful enough to bring a halt to the despicable acts. It seems to us that the I.D.F. should continue to foster the [consciousness of] basic moral obligations which must be kept even in war conditions, without prejudicing the I.D.F.'s combat ability. The circumstances of combat require the combatants to be tough—which means to give priority to sticking to the objective and being willing to make sacrifices—in order to attain the objectives assigned to them, even under the most difficult conditions. But the end never justifies the means, and basic ethical and human values must be maintained in the use of arms.

Among the responses to the commission from the public, there were those who expressed dissatisfaction with the holding of an inquiry on a subject not directly related to Israel's responsibility. The argument was advanced that in previous instances of massacre in Lebanon, when the lives of many more people were taken than those of the victims who fell in Sabra and Shatilla, world opinion was not shocked and no inquiry commissions were established. We cannot justify this approach to the issue of holding an inquiry, and not only for the formal reason that it was not we who decided to hold the inquiry, but rather the Israeli Government resolved thereon. The main purpose of the inquiry was to bring to light all the important facts relating to the perpetration of the atrocities; it therefore has importance from the perspective of Israel's moral fortitude and its functioning as a democratic state that scrupulously maintains the fundamental principles of the civilized world.

We do not deceive ourselves that the results of this inquiry will convince or satisfy those who have prejudices or selective consciences, but this inquiry was not intended for such people. We have striven and have spared no effort to arrive at the truth, and we hope that all persons of good will who will examine the issue without prejudice will be convinced that the inquiry was conducted without any bias.

PUBLICATION
OF THE REPORT

In accordance with Section 20(a) of the Commissions of Inquiry Law, this report and the attached Appendix A will be published after the report is submitted to the Government. Appendix B to this report will not be published, since we are convinced that this is necessary to protect the security of the state and its foreign relations.

Transcripts from the commission hearings which were conducted in open session have already been made public. In accordance with regulation 8(b) of the Commission of Inquiry Regulations (Rules of Procedure) 1969, we resolve that the right to examine the transcripts from those sessions which were held in camera, as well as Appendix B to the report, will be given to all members of the Cabinet, all members of the Knesset Defense and Foreign Affairs Committee, the General Staff of the Israel Defense Forces, and any person or class of persons which may be determined by the Ministerial Defense Committee. Similarly, the right to examine Appendix B is given to those persons who received a notice in accordance with section 15(a) of the law, and to their representatives who appeared before the commission.

This report was signed on 7 February 1983.

Yitzhak Kahan   **Aharon Barak**   **Yona Efrat**
Commission Chairman   Commission Member   Commission Member

Translated by Bezalel Gordon, Ralph Mandel,
Ina Friedman, Joel Greenberg, Nancy Wellins,
on behalf of the Government Press Office.

APPENDICES

APPENDIX A

SECTION 1

**Resolution of the Commission of
Inquiry Investigating the Events of
the Refugee Camps in Beirut, 24.11.82**
This resolution is issued by the commission in accordance with the instructions of Section 15 of the Commissions of Inquiry Law, 5728-1969, which stipulates:

15. (A) Where it appears to a commission of inquiry that a particular person is likely to be harmed by the inquiry or by its results, the chairman of the commission shall notify that person in what respect he is likely to be harmed and shall place at his disposal, in such manner as he may think fit, such evidence relevant to that potential harm as is in the possession of the commission or of a person entrusted with the collection of material under Section 13.

(B) A person notified under subsection (A) may attend before the commission either himself or through an advocate, make statements and examine witnesses (even if they have already testified before the commission), and the commission may permit him to present evidence, all in relation to the said potential harm.

(C) A person at whose disposal evidence has been placed under subsection (A) shall not publish any part thereof without the prior approval of the commission.

(D) Despite what is said in subsection (A), the commission of inquiry is permitted not to notify that person as said there, on the condition that it is convinced that nothing in the conduct of the inquiry is harmful to him, and that in its report it will not determine findings or conclusions regarding him, and will not make recommendations regarding him.

After examination of the evidence which we have heard and of the other material in our possession, we determine that harm could be caused by this inquiry or its results, as will be enumerated in this decision.

1. The Prime Minister, Mr. Menachem Begin, may be harmed if the commission arrives at the following findings or conclusions:
   A) That the Prime Minister did not appropriately consider the role to be played by the Lebanese Forces during and due to the I.D.F.'s entry into West Beirut, and ignored the danger of acts of revenge and bloodshed by these Forces against the population in the refugee camps.
   B) That the aforementioned omission is tantamount to non-fulfillment of a duty which was incumbent on the Prime Minister.

2. The Minister of Defense, Mr. Ariel Sharon, may be harmed if the commission determines the following findings or conclusions:
   A) That the Minister of Defense ignored or disregarded the danger of acts of revenge and bloodshed by the Lebanese Forces against the population in the refugee camps in Beirut, and did not order that the appropriate measures be taken to prevent this danger.
   B) That the Minister of Defense did not order that the Lebanese Forces be removed from the camps as quickly as possible, and that steps be taken to protect the population in the camps, when he received reports of acts of killing or acts which deviate from regular combat operations which were carried out in the refugee camps under the control of the Lebanese Forces.
   C) That the aforementioned omission is tantamount to non-fulfillment of a duty incumbent on the Minister of Defense.

3. The Minister of Foreign Affairs, Mr. Yitzhak Shamir, may be harmed if the commission determines the following findings or conclusions:
   A) That the Foreign Minister, after hearing from Minister Zipori on 17.9.82 the report on the actions of the Lebanese Forces in the refugee camps, took no appropriate step to clarify whether this report had grounds, and did not bring the report to the knowledge of the Prime Minister or Defense Minister.
   B) That the aforementioned omission is tantamount to non-fulfillment of a duty incumbent on the Foreign Minister.

4. The Chief of Staff, Lieutenant General Rafael Eitan, may be harmed if the commission determines the following findings or conclusions:
   A) That the Chief of Staff ignored or dismissed from his mind the danger of acts of revenge and bloodshed by the Lebanese Forces

against the population in the refugee camps in Beirut, and did not order that appropriate measures be taken to prevent this danger.

B) That the Chief of Staff, when reports reached him of acts of killing or acts which deviate from regular combat operations which were carried out in the refugee camps under the control of the Lebanese Forces, did not check the veracity of the reports and the scope of the acts, and did not order the cessation of the actions of the Lebanese Forces in the camps, their removal from the camps as quickly as possible, and the taking of measures to protect the population in the camps.

C) That the Chief of Staff, in a meeting with the commanders of the Lebanese Forces which was held on 17.9.82 and after this meeting, approved the continuation of the Lebanese Forces' operation in the refugee camps until 18.9.82 and ordered that they be given assistance for the continuation of their actions.

D) That the aforementioned omission constitutes a breach of duty or non-fulfillment of a duty which was incumbent on the Chief of Staff.

5. The director of Military Intelligence, Maj.-Gen. Yehoshua Saguy, may be harmed if the commission determines the following findings or conclusions:

A) That the director of Military Intelligence did not give proper attention to the decision taken regarding the role which the Lebanese Forces would play during the I.D.F.'s entry into West Beirut, and did not warn after the murder of Bashir Jemayel of the danger of acts of revenge and bloodshed by these Forces against the Palestinian population in West Beirut, and especially against the population in the refugee camps.

B) That the director of Military Intelligence did not as quickly as possible bring to the knowledge of the Prime Minister, the Defense Minister, and the Chief of Staff the report which he had received on Friday, 17.9.82, in the morning hours, about what had occurred in the refugee camps under the control of the Lebanese Forces.

C) That the aforementioned omission is tantamount to non-fulfillment of a duty which was incumbent on the director of Military Intelligence.

6. The director of the Institution for Intelligence and Special Projects [Mossad] may be harmed if the commission determines the following findings or conclusions:

A) That the director of the Mossad did not give proper attention to

the decision taken regarding the role to be played by the Lebanese Forces during the I.D.F.'s entry into West Beirut, and did not warn after the murder of Bashir Jemayel of the danger of acts of revenge and bloodshed by these Forces against the Palestinian population in West Beirut, and especially against the population in the refugee camps.
B) That the aforementioned omission is tantamount to non-fulfillment of a duty which was incumbent on the head of the Mossad.

7. The G.O.C. Northern Command, Amir Drori, may be harmed if the commission determines the following findings or conclusions:
A) That the G.O.C. did not take appropriate and sufficient steps to prevent the continuation of actions by the Lebanese Forces in the refugee camps, when he received reports of acts of murder or acts which deviate from regular combat operations which were carried out in the refugee camps under the control of the Lebanese Forces.
B) That the G.O.C. did not warn the Chief of Staff, when said arrived in Beirut on 17.9.82, of the danger posed to the population in the camps by the continued activity or presence of the Lebanese Forces in the camps, and did not try to prevent the continuation of this activity in a meeting with the commanders of the Lebanese Forces which was held on 17.9.82, or shortly thereafter.
C) That the aforementioned omission is tantamount to non-fulfillment of a duty incumbent on the G.O.C.

8. Brig.-Gen. Amos Yaron may be harmed if the commission determines the following findings or conclusions:
A) That Brig.-Gen. Yaron did not appropriately evaluate and did not check the reports received regarding acts of killing or acts deviating from regular combat operations by the Lebanese Forces in the refugee camps, and did not report to the G.O.C. and the Chief of Staff on these reports and their significance immediately after they were transmitted to him on 16.9.82, in the evening hours or in the early hours of the night.
B) That Brig.-Gen. Yaron did not take appropriate steps to stop the actions of the Lebanese Forces in West Beirut and to protect the population in the camps, immediately upon hearing the reports referred to in the above paragraph (A).
C) That Brig.-Gen. Yaron did not warn the Chief of Staff, when the latter arrived in Beirut on 17.9.82, of the danger posed to the population in the camps by the continued activity or presence of the Lebanese Forces in the camps, and gave the Lebanese Forces

approval to send a new force into the camps without taking steps which would ensure the cessation of the irregular actions of these Forces in the refugee camps.

D) That the aforementioned omission constitutes a breach of duty or non-fulfillment of a duty which was incumbent on Brig.-Gen. Yaron.

9. Mr. Avi Duda'i, Personal Aide to the Defense Minister, may be harmed if the commission determines the following findings or conclusions.

A) That Mr. Duda'i received on 17.9.82, in the morning hours, or before noon, a report of acts of killing which had been carried out by the Lebanese Forces in the refugee camps and did not transmit this report to the Minister of Defense.

B) That the aforementioned omission is tantamount to non-fulfillment of a duty which was incumbent on the Personal Aide to the Defense Minister.

The Chairman of the Commission will inform those who may be harmed by the inquiry or its results, in accordance with the instructions of Section 15 (A) above, of the aforementioned harm.

This Resolution adopted on 8 Kislev, 5743 (24.11.82)

YITZHAK KAHAN   AHARON BARAK   YONA EFRAT
COMMISSION CHAIRMAN

SECTION 2

Stages in Operation
Peace for Galilee
(Exhibit 214)

1. 6 June	—Start of the operation
2. 10 June	—Fighting on outskirts of Beirut from the south.
3. 12-14 June	—Takeover of Beirut suburbs (Khaldeh, Kafr Shuma, Ba'abda) and linkup with Christians.
4. 14 June	—Philip Habib arrives for first round of talks with Sarkis on a ceasefire and settlement.
5. 16 June	—The P.L.O. announces its readiness to conduct negotiations with Habib, and the indirect negotiations through Lebanon get under way.
6. 23 June	—The P.L.O. presents its "5-point" plan for a settlement in Beirut.

7. 25 June	—Completion of encirclement of Beirut and take-over of the Suk-al-Arab-Aley area (Beirut-Damascus road).
8. 5 July	—Start of search to find recipient states for the evacuated terrorists.
9. 10 July	—The P.L.O. presents its "11-point" plan for a settlement in Beirut.
10. 31 July-1 Aug.	—Capture of the airport at Khaldeh.
11. 2-3 Aug.	—Capture of Uzai.
12. 3 Aug.	—The P.L.O. presents a plan for total evacuation and substantive concessions to Habib.
13. 4-5 Aug.	—I.D.F. enters the Hippodrome.
14. 7 Aug.	—The P.L.O. presents a plan for the evacuation of 7,100 terrorists from Beirut within two weeks.
15. 9 Aug.	—Heavy I.D.F. artillery fire on Beirut and terrorist targets.
16. 10 Aug.	—Syrian readiness to receive the terrorists.
17. 12 Aug.	—Massive air force attack on Beirut.
18. 19 Aug.	—Completion of the negotiations on the evacuation of the terrorists from Beirut.
19. 23 Aug.	—Bashir Jemayel elected president.
20. 21-26 Aug.	—Arrival of the multinational force and start of the evacuation of the terrorists.
21. 1 Sept.	—Completion of terrorists' evacuation.
22. 10-12 Sept.	—Multinational force leaves Beirut.
23. 14 Sept.	—Assassination of Bashir.
24. 15 Sept.	—I.D.F. enters West Beirut.
25. 16 Sept.	—Phalangists enter refugee camps.

APPENDIX B
(SECRET)

PARLIAMENTARY ADDRESSES OF 22.9.82

ADDRESS OF DEFENSE
MINISTER ARIEL SHARON

This is a dark day for all of us. Innocent people, old men, women and children were murdered for no crime in Beirut. In the cruelest possible way.

The human mind cannot accept that such would be the fate of innocent people. I did not come to explain this terrible tragedy, because it is part of a nether world, not ours, but of those who perpetrated this slaughter. I hope they get their just punishment, although this is not under our control.

I came here to report on the matters for which we are responsible, and only on these will I speak. They have no connection whatsoever, in any shape or form, with the criminal acts of murder. For we are not at war with the Palestinian people.

We have declared a war of destruction on Palestinian terror. And if there are those indirectly responsible for these acts of murder—those directly responsible are Lebanese—then those indirectly responsible belong to the P.L.O. terror organization. Therefore, I can say clearly and immediately that no soldier and no commander in the Israel Defense Forces participated in this terrible act. The hands of the I.D.F. are clean.

When we agreed to the entry of the Phalangists to the refugee camps, senior commanders distinctly told them, and I quote, that a military force would be allowed into the Shatilla camp to seek out and destroy terrorists. In the coordinating meetings, it was stressed that the action was to be against terrorists and not to harm the civilian population, and especially women, children and the elderly, endquote.

The following are excerpts from the text of Defense Minister Ariel Sharon's address to Parliament on September 22, 1982 in defense of the army's role in the Beirut massacre. The text is translated from the Hebrew by The New York Times. *Some interruptions from the floor are shown in brackets.*

Interrogation of Commanders

The moment a question arose as to what was happening in the camps, which we recognized as centers of terrorism in West Beirut, the chief of the northern command took immediate steps to halt the action of the Phalangists in Shatilla by immediately contacting a liaison officer of the Phalangists who was at our regional headquarters. We have to remember that the Phalangists are not the I.D.F. Their units and their men are not under our command.

And they do not have to report to us. In this sad affair, our senior officer at the scene stubbornly asked the Phalangists for details and asked again and again for reports from Phalangist officers: "What did your men say? What did your men do?" We spared no effort. The northern commander, the Chief of Staff and myself went up there in order to interrogate their commanders, in order to understand and to know that, when and why this tragedy occurred. But these people refuse to this very day to talk. They are not even willing to admit to the act. We ourselves were forced to try—and are still checking and trying to find out—why they did this in violation of their commitment given to us, in violation of our demand.

And if by any chance Mr. Peres would care to listen, Mr. Peres who is so worked up over an incident that occurred without our knowledge, let me say that I can remind him of an affair that took place during his time and with his foreknowledge.

[Calls from legislators: Sharon should resign! Sharon should resign!]

Therefore, this whole experience whereby you take every opportunity, and in the ears of the whole world, to incite against, to pour oil on the fire . . .

[Micha Harish, Labor: You are responsible, Mr. Defense Minister!]

You would certainly like me to resign. The Americans, too, as I've read in recent days, would like to see me resign.

[Jacques Amir, Labor: Why?]

Not only do you want to replace me; the Americans also want to replace me. But there is a difference in the reasons why you, who toady up to the Americans, want to replace me and why the Americans want to replace me. You want to replace me because you want these seats here [pointing to Cabinet's chairs in center of the chamber] around this table. The Americans want to replace me not because their objective is Beirut, but because their objective is Jerusalem, their objective is Hebron, their objective is Beit El. Their objective is Elon Moreh and Ariel. And you, in your collaboration, are deliberately lending a hand to the replacement of Israel, in order to get to power with the help of others, and to give up parts of the land of Israel. You, your objective is this table. Them, their objective is there [gesturing outside toward the West Bank]. You, in linking up with them, are helping them to implement the comprehensive solution presented to us, which is handing over parts of the land of Israel. You will not succeed. Therefore, any attempt to attribute this sad chapter to the I.D.F., including a call to appoint a commission of inquiry, all this is committing an injustice to the I.D.F.

[Amnon Rubinstein, Shinui Party: It's you who should be investigated!]

We are ready to be investigated on everything. There is no problem, but all this is an injustice to the Israel Defense Forces, which are in our charge.

The right address is the Phalangists, not the I.D.F. Nobody here is trying to hide anything. Our Government, like all our people, is sensitive to acts of terror, more so than any other government or any other people in the world.

The I.D.F., its soldiers and commanders, have been performing for three months a wonderful operation in Lebanon, which has brought and will bring great security gains. Every movement of our soldiers was known to us and was reported immediately. That is the tragedy of the camps. We did not know exactly what was taking place.

Phalangists in the Camps
[Several labor backbenchers: Lies, lies, all lies!]

And until today we do not know exactly, because when the acts took place the Phalangists were in the camps, and they are not soldiers of the I.D.F. The soldiers of the I.D.F. and its commanders did not go into these camps under express orders.

There were rumors, partial reports. And when the picture became clear, when we saw the enormity of the tragedy, it was too late, too late to do anything, although we intervened at the rise of the first suspicions. And I want to ask Parliament Member Peres, who stood here before me with disgusting self-righteousness attacking us for something we knew nothing about, I want to ask you, Shimon Peres, you in your time—and with foreknowledge—there was another affair. And I would not bring it up except that you have sunk to the lowest rung of the ladder.

When you were Defense Minister, there was an affair in Tell Zaatar. When you were Defense Minister. I will not go into details here. How come your conscience does not bother you? Thousands of people were slaughtered. And Parliament Member Peres, where were the officers of the I.D.F. on that day, and that was an affair that occurred with foreknowledge.

[Peres: Why are you lying again? The Speaker tells him he will have a chance to respond later.]

123

Were you shocked then? You knew about it.

There is a limit to everything even for those of you who have no share in the national interest. You cannot make charges about something which took place without our knowledge. We did not know. Would that we had known.

I am going to read to you from an official document of ours, and I want to stress that as soon as I learned of the outrage, I asked for the preparation of official reports on what occurred. And to the extent that it was possible to obtain testimony as to what took place. Therefore I want to report to you what happened from our standpoint, according to an official military report. I will read the portions that touch on our discussion.

First, the Phalangists entered the refugee camp of Shatilla on the night of the 16th of September, 1982, and their activities were halted by the I.D.F. on the 17th in the afternoon, after rumors reached us as to what was occurring in the camp. The area was completely evacuated by Saturday the 18th of September in the hours before noon.

Secondly, in the wake of the murder of Bashir Jemayel, a decision was taken that the I.D.F. should gain control of key areas in West Beirut.

The decision was that the northern command should get control of key areas in the western part of the city. This decision was taken on the 15th of September at 12:30 A.M.

Thirdly, this operation was carried out from the 15th of September 1982 beginning with the afternoon hours, starting at 5:00 P.M., and ended on Thursday in the afternoon, with the emphasis being on not hurting civilian residents and their property. And indeed, there were almost no civilian casualties or damage to their property.

Fourth, in a decision reached by the command, it was forbidden absolutely to go into the refugee camps. Search-and-destroy missions will be carried out by the Phalangists or the Army of Lebanon.

Fifth, on the 15th of September, after the murder of Bashir Jemayel, at 3:30 P.M., a meeting was carried out with the Phalangist command in which the Chief of Staff and northern commander participated, and during which we discussed the operations of the Phalangists and the entry of the I.D.F. into the western part of the city.

And we spoke in principle of their dealing with the camps.

Sixth, on Wednesday the 15th, in the afternoon hours, we received an absolutely negative response from the army of Lebanon in response to our request that the army of Lebanon enter the camps.

Seventh, on Wednesday the 15th in the evening hours, the northern commander met with the commander of the Phalangists and with Col.

Michel On, the head of the Lebanese Army units in Beirut, in which the northern commander pressed the Lebanese colonel to persuade the political echelons in the Lebanese Government to approve the entry of the army of Lebanon into the camps.

Eight. After checking, the Lebanese officer claimed that it was impossible and that in a meeting with the Prime Minister of Lebanon he was told that he was under orders to open fire on Israeli soldiers entering West Beirut, and he was threatened with a court martial.

Entry of Phalangists

Nine. Once again on Thursday the 16th of September, the army of Lebanon passed a negative response to the possibility that the army of Lebanon would go into the camps.

Ten. On the 16th of September in the afternoon, a meeting was held between the northern commander and the commander of the Phalangists with regard to several matters, and on the same day in the afternoon a meeting was held between the division commander in the area and the representative of the Phalangists to coordinate the entry of the Phalangists into the camp of Shatilla.

Eleven. The agreement was that the Phalangists would enter the camp from the south and the west to search out terrorist nests. In the coordinating meeting it was stressed that the operation was against terrorists, and that it was forbidden to harm the civilian population, especially women, children and the elderly.

Twelve. On the night of the 16th of September, a force of the Phalangists entered Shatilla camp. As per their request they got at a certain time flares fired from 81 millimeter mortars and flares from planes.

Thirteen. On the 17th of September, 1982, the Phalangists concentrated a force of infantry, artillery and medical personnel in order to continue the mopping-up in the camps.

Fourteen. The I.D.F. prevented the entry of this force as part of the operation in the camps.

Fifteen. On Friday the 17th around noon—actually around 11 A.M.—the division commander met with the northern commander. The division commander raised suspicions concerning the method of operation of the Phalangists. Even then it was not known what was going on in Shatilla camp. The northern commander ordered the immediate halt of the Phalangist activities, by means of the Phalangist liaison officer at the headquarters.

Sixteen. On Friday the 17th at 4:30 P.M., a meeting was held with the Phalangist staff and the Chief of Staff and the northern commander, in which it was agreed that all the Phalangists would leave the refugee camps on Saturday morning, the 18th of September. It was also agreed that no further forces would enter the camps. At this meeting as well, the events in Shatilla camp were still not known.

Seventeen. On Friday the 17th of September in the evening, an official announcement was received from the army of Lebanon after a meeting of the Lebanese Government that the army of Lebanon would not go into the camps.

Eighteen. On the 18th of September in the morning, the Phalangist forces left the areas of the refugee camps. And then news began to arrive about the events in the Shatilla camp. As a result of this, the northern commander ordered that the I.D.F. enter the camp of Fakhani.

What the I.D.F. Knew
And on Sunday the 19th in the morning, into the Sabra camp as well, in order to protect the population and put them at ease, the population which greeted the I.D.F. warmly. Likewise, the northern commander was ordered not to go into Shatilla camp so that the I.D.F. would not be linked to the events that occurred there. Then, we still did not know who would link the I.D.F. to these events. We never thought that you would be the ones doing the linking.

This sounds to you, and rightfully, like a laconic and dry report, but this is what the I.D.F. knew and did.

I did not come here today to claim that some person or another did not see more, did not hear more than is written in this report. But this was the picture that crystallized in the headquarters of the northern command and in the general staff headquarters. We should always remember that it was not we who entered Shatilla camp, but the Phalangists.

We did not imagine in our worst dreams that the Phalangists would act thus, as they entered the battle at this time of the war. They looked like a regular army in all respects. They promised to fight only against the terrorists. We had a good experience with them in the past, when during the siege of Beirut, they conquered the Faculty of Sciences, the neighborhood of Reihan, and Jamhour. In addition, they were active in policing the road blocks between the two parts of the city. And they carried out their operations with efficiency. We passed along to them responsibility over various areas which we conquered, and they generally performed—and I emphasize generally, because there were a few mishaps—in good fashion, except for a few small exceptions.

We consented to the entry of the Phalangists in order to save the lives of our soldiers, although we never imagined in our worst dreams that these same Phalangists would do the worst thing possible. It is possible that you will come and say that this was an error in judgment in estimating the situation. But I do not say that. And I want you to pay attention.

Comment on the War

Three weeks after the start of the war a noted person came to me and said, "Lord in heaven, what are the Phalangists doing, they who are our allies in this matter? They told us that at some point the Christians would enter Beirut. After all it is their capital. They too have to do something to liberate their homeland. What's their part in this war? Is their part only that they sprinkle rice on our soldiers and hand out flowers, while we give blood? After all, did not we the Alignment [the Labor and Mapam parties] open up the path for the Christians to power when we were in the Government?"

When I saw this I said, Lord in heaven, is this someone from the Agudath or the National Religious Party? No. This was the respected member of Parliament Mr. Victor Shemtov. He came to me with this claim. Member of Parliament Victor Shemtov. Just as Mr. Shemtov was right in his claim that the Alignment opened up the way for the Christians, so we have continued in your path with boldness. The Government headed by Menachem Begin. And can we choose our neighbors in the Middle East?

Throughout all these months, I was continually asked, "Why don't the Phalangists fight within Beirut? Why do their hands remain clean?"

You cannot have it both ways. You cannot harp on the fact that the Phalangists do not join the fighting, and then the moment a terrible tragedy happens, for which we are not responsible, roll your righteous eyes heavenward. The interesting thing is that after the slaughter of the Moslems by the Christians a few days ago, there is already a consensus in Lebanon, but here each one tears at the flesh of his neighbor. And for what? Why? About what? About what we did not do.

You are throwing oil on the fire. You are throwing oil on the fire of anti-Semitism. A bonfire of blood libels.

And I would like to tell you that after we went into West Beirut, we found in the terrorists' command post, material. Let me tell you about what we found during the war. I want to tell you about an organized campaign being carried out to overturn the Government by those in the opposition and by some in the media. They want a commission of inquiry? They are seeking the overturn of the Government. King Hussein, too, wants a new government. He wants you, and he knows why.

The Reagan Plan

From the first day the Likud came to power and during the difficult and necessary days of the war—the war of defense in Lebanon—you did not cease even for an instant. And today many of the putsch-makers, directly and indirectly, are aiding those within the American Administration who decided to dictate the Reagan plan to us, and also to replace the Government.

And yesterday in *The New York Times* there was a report that Reagan and his advisers in large measure would like to see changes in the Israeli Government. *The New York Times* is a serious newspaper, but fortunately Washington does not appoint, inaugurate or fire ministers or governments in Israel. Not Washington. Members of the Parliament, whether you be in the coalition or the opposition: This is Jerusalem, not Saigon. It would be well for you to remember this. How has such a choir of poison and hatred arisen among us? Self-hatred like this, to suggest that we are guilty of the massacre in Beirut.

A Secret Inquiry

It became known to me how much the leaders of the P.L.O. built their resistance during the siege upon the divisions of opinion in Israel. They tied their hopes to this. The heads of the P.L.O. in their discussions arrived at the following conclusions: when they saw the confusion in Israel, and I will quote—and for this we will be ready for a commission of inquiry—and to make it easy for you we will make it a secret commission of inquiry, in order to make it easy for you.

I tell you with all responsibility that the war in Beirut stretched out longer because of the irresponsible attacks on the Government. And this is certainly the subject for a commission of inquiry. And I am ready for it to be conducted behind closed doors. We will supply the data and you will learn the damage you caused.

We succeeded despite these attempts against the Government to consolidate our positions in Lebanon, to enhance our gains, and above all, at this moment, we are continuing the mopping-up operations and the collection of spoils from the centers of terror in West Beirut, and by so doing, we will complete this unprecedented operation of expelling the terror organizations from Beirut. The final step, which you attacked here, began last Tuesday. As you know, we never wanted to go into West Beirut.

But dramatic developments forced our hand.

You will surely understand why letting the Phalangists into the camps while the Lebanese Army refused to go in was a natural step in order to prevent loss of life in our forces. The inhuman tragedy which took place was beyond our control, notwithstanding all the pain and the sorrow. We cannot bear the responsibility on our shoulders. We are continuing to check and study various details on the state of coordination, supervision among our forces. But we will do so carefully.

I am coming now to the stage of the withdrawal of all the foreign forces from Lebanon. We are coming now to the stage of withdrawing all the foreign forces from Lebanon. And by doing that we will advance toward the final goal: peace and security with Lebanon. This is within our reach, especially if we cease to spread blood libels about ourselves, and if we take a joint stand.

ADDRESS OF LABOR PARTY
LEADER SHIMON PERES

Members of Parliament, it is not with a light heart that I address you. At this time, perhaps more than ever before, the Jewish nation stands before its conscience. Not because of what the Gentiles say and not because of what the newspapers write, but because of the growing fear that arises from the depths of our heritage.

We have a sense that underneath the blocks of cement used to cover the bodies of children, women and old men, lie moral ruins. The chief rabbis have so attested, seeing that the slaughter of hundreds of innocent men, women and children in the refugee camps of Sabra and Shatilla in Beirut were conducted by the lowest form of murderers, people who have lost their divine spark, their human image. We all confront this abominable act, which the rabbis said is the absolute antithesis of the traditions of Judaism. The ground trembles beneath our feet, and from all classes is heard a painful cry of disapproval.

But the Prime Minister and the Defense Minister were struck dumb. Their silence thundered as it pained. The fate of Israel, David Ben-Gurion said, is dependent on its strength and its righteousness. Righteousness, not just strength, have to guide our deeds.

In May 1981 Menachem Begin said: We are a Jewish state, with our experiences. We will not agree under any circumstances to any attempt by the Syrians to turn the Christians during the 1980s into the Jews of Europe from the 1940s. I want to believe the Prime Minister, that that was appropriate not only for Jews, not only for Christians, but also for Moslems. Children are children, whether they are Jews, Arabs or Lebanese. Their blood is red and worthy of respect, irrespective of race or religion. All share man's image. The blood of all is holy in our eyes.

The following are excerpts from the text of Labor Party leader Shimon Peres's address to Parliament on September 22, 1982.

Israel Facing Itself

The question that stands before us, the Government, the opposition, the whole nation, is the question of Israel facing itself, Israel facing its history. Israel with the truth of its experience. And anyone who tries to gloss over this truth because of a suspicion, "What will the non-Jews say?" is sinning against Israel, is sinning against the sense by which Israel was founded. Those who try to hush the voices will not help.

I do not suggest for a second that anybody in Israel would knowingly lend his hand, directly or indirectly, to this shocking criminal act. And even as I come to call this Government and its head to account, I must make clear that I do not accuse them of premeditated connections in any way to this heinous deed. And in the name of the unity of the nation I call upon all members of this house to exclude the Israel Defense Forces from this discussion. Let us leave aside our sons who are serving their nation faithfully. Let us not include the great and important organization that carries out orders, and which is blameless altogether: let us leave them out of this painful political controversy. We are sure that the Israel Defense Forces did not lend its hand to this spilling of blood.

Nevertheless, there is no way to pass over the heavy sins of the Government, which did not pay attention to the obvious state of things; grave mistakes in judgment, closing its ears to warnings, and which because of lack of ability or lack of will tries to shake off the burden of responsibility for its actions and its failures.

There are things in this affair that should be brought before a judicial inquiry, but there are things that are visible to the eye, clear as day. There is no reason to gloss over them or to hide them. The first is the penetration into West Beirut. We warned publicly again and again that we should not under any circumstances go into this large city, torn by factional strife, amid a blood feud and trembling from historical tensions.

The Question of Arms

What is our connection to Beirut, Mr. Prime Minister? The arms caches? And if we take out the arms, who among us can be sure that after some time, other implements of war will not be smuggled in, perhaps more advanced? Is there a shortage of armaments in the world? Will we control Beirut forever in order to prevent this? Is there any sort of guarantee that the local authorities who come in afterwards will want or be able to prevent the transfer of substitute arms?

Is this the only Arab capital with armaments? Who so decided? Two men, the Prime Minister and the Defense Minister. How did they explain this? According to a news item published in Maariv on the first of the month they said it was the desire to prevent the danger of violence, bloodshed, chaos. But, as is their custom, they hurried to pat themselves on the back, and they put their announcement in the following historic words: "This objective indeed was achieved."

What flippancy, Mr. Prime Minister. What have you wrought, Mr. Prime Minister and Mr. Defense Minister? When you took upon yourselves the public responsibility for what was liable to happen in Beirut, what did you cause? When you announced that all the strategic junctions were in our hands, that the refugee camps were besieged on all sides, under our supervision. If you indeed estimated what was liable to occur and you were not able to prevent it, then it is a terrible failure. And if you didn't know what was liable to be the result of your unfortunate decision on Sunday night, then it is a mortal danger to entrust in your hands further decisions of this scope.

And the contention that if we were not there, worse things would have happened is unfortunate and dangerous. Did you decide to go into West Beirut because you saw that less serious things would occur—in other words, something not serious enough? The Prime Minister came out with one of his bits of wisdom in the Cabinet meeting yesterday: The Gentiles kill the Gentiles, and now they come to hang the Jews. If the Gentiles are killing the Gentiles, Mr. Prime Minister, why did you inject the Jews into this problem? Who asked you? This hurried decision was taken in the aftermath of the murder of Bashir Jemayel. Were we responsible for his election? Are we capable of sustaining the results of his murder?

Bashir Jemayel's Election
Bashir Jemayel was elected by the laws and precepts of Lebanon, and there only. Partly because of his record and partly despite his record. And just as we were were not involved in his election, or should not have been seen as involved in his election, so we should not, we must not be involved or be seen to be involved in the state of things created by the murder of the President-elect of Lebanon, and the acts of vengeance in its wake.

Who in Lebanon will investigate these acts? Who in Lebanon will want to investigate this murder and acts of vengeance? Don't you know that there is a convenient way to roll all the charges and accusations onto someone at the first opportune moment? Lebanon lived without us. There is a Lebanese Army. There was a possibility of restoring the multinational force. Why did we have to burden our soldiers with danger and bring indirectly on ourselves—with complete blindness—a responsibility that we cannot bear? The meeting between the Prime

Minister, the Defense Minister, the Foreign Minister and Bashir Jemayel Sunday night was a cardinal mistake. Nobody has to ask, Mr. Begin, what men do at night. But the affairs themselves should have taken into account the timing, to take into account that they might be leaked to the public, as they were, and would not add honor the next morning to Israel or security the next evening to Lebanon or its new President. But he who travels too quickly without paying attention to the path is bound to have his mistake redound to greater proportions than he expected.

And when the I.D.F. got orders to enter West Beirut, I want to ask, Mr. Prime Minister, Mr. Defense Minister, whose was this stupid idea, to send the Phalangists to the refugee camps to find the terrorists? Do you have an answer, Mr. Sharon? You don't have to be a political genius or a decorated general, it's enough to be a village policeman to understand ahead of time that these militias—in the wake of the murder of their leader—were more liable than ever to sow destruction, even among innocent people. Is this surprising? This was something unprecedented? And if the Government approved on Thursday night the 16th, the entry into the camps by the Phalangists, then where was your supervision? Where were your reports? Where was your follow through? The television photographers had to unearth this?

BIOGRAPHIES OF THE KAHAN
COMMISSION MEMBERS

Yitzhak Kahan, *President of the Supreme Court*   Born on November 15, 1913 into a Hasidic family in Brody, Poland, Yitzhak Kahan moved to Palestine in 1935 after graduating from Poland's University of Lwow with two master's degrees—one in law and another in economics and administration. In 1940, Mr. Kahan obtained his license to practice law in Palestine and was a lawyer in Haifa for the next ten years, becoming a municipal judge in Haifa in 1950. During the war of independence in 1948, Mr. Kahan served in the Israeli Army. In 1953, he was appointed to the District Court, where he served until his appointment to the Supreme Court, becoming Chief Justice of the Supreme Court in 1982. A deeply religious man who has shown reluctance to interfere in executive and legislative matters, Mr. Kahan at the same time has a record of uncompromising commitment to judicial independence and is known for his balanced and concise legal opinions.

Aharon Barak, *Justice of the Supreme Court*   Currently 46 years of age and a specialist in commercial law, Aharon Barak has consistently defended individual rights against the prerogatives of the state. As Attorney General in 1977, Mr. Barak sent to prison the government's nominee for chairman of the Bank of Israel and also forced the minister of finance to withdraw a proposal granting amnesty to tax evaders. He was responsible for indictments against leading figures in the ruling Labor party for financial wrongdoing and in April 1977 prosecuted Prime Minister Yitzhak Rabin's wife for holding a US bank account, which ultimately led to Yitzhak Rabin's resignation. As Prime Minister Menachem Begin's legal adviser in 1978 during the Camp David negotiations, Mr. Barak's careful formulations were responsible for repeatedly breaking deadlocks. Mr. Barak joined the Supreme Court soon after the Camp David talks.

Yonah Efrat, *Major General (Res.), Israel Defense Forces*   Member of the Haganah (Jewish militia) in Palestine before the establishment of

Israel and wounded in the war of independence, Yonah Efrat rose through the army ranks to head the central command. He has served on several commissions of inquiry into possible army misconduct, including a 1978 official inquiry into a guerrilla attack that left 36 Jewish civilians, who were on a bus, dead. Mr. Efrat is retired from the army and currently heads a private company.